SUBVERTING POLITICS
AUTONOMOUS SOCIAL MOVEMENTS TODAY

MARCOS ANCELOVICI
FRANCIS DUPUIS-DÉRI, eds.

**BLACK
ROSE
BOOKS**

Montréal · New York · London

Black Rose Books No. WW434

Library and Archives Canada Cataloguing in Publication

Title: Subverting politics : autonomous social movements today / Marcos Ancelovici & Francis Dupuis-Déri, eds.
Names: Ancelovici, Marcos, editor. | Dupuis-Déri, Francis, 1966- editor.
Description: Includes bibliographical references.
Identifiers: Canadiana (print) 20220470960 | Canadiana (ebook) 20220470995 | ISBN 9781551648026 (hardcover) | ISBN 9781551648002 (softcover) | ISBN 9781551648040 (PDF)
Subjects: LCSH: Social movements. | LCSH: Political activists. | LCSH: Power (Social sciences) | LCSH: Autonomy.
Classification: LCC HM881 .S83 2023 | DDC 303.48/4—dc23

Cover photo of an autonomous squat in Madrid, Spain by Juan Luis Sotillo. Cover design by Associés Libres Design.

BLACK
ROSE
BOOKS

C.P. 42002 Succ. Roy
Montréal, QC H2W 2T3
CANADA
www.blackrosebooks.com

ORDERING INFORMATION

CANADA / USA	UK / INTERNATIONAL
University of Toronto Press 5201 Dufferin Street Toronto, ON M3H 5T8 1-800-565-9523 utpbooks@utpress.utoronto.ca	Central Books 50 Freshwater Road Chadwell Heath, London RM8 1RX +44 20 85 25 8800 contactus@centralbooks.com

Table of Contents

Acknowledgements

This book is the result of a two-day workshop that we organized at l'Université du Québec à Montréal (UQAM) in April 2017. In addition to George Katsiaficas, who traveled all the way from South Korea to attend the event, it brought together Richard Day, Émeline Fourment, Jason Del Gandio, Anna Kruzynski, and Rachel Sarrasin. It was a stimulating and warm meeting, during which intellectual and political affinities joyfully overlapped. Robert Lovelace, Miguel Martínez, and AK Thompson joined us afterward with additional contributions that shed light on other dimensions of autonomous struggles. We wish to thank all the contributors for their work as well as Marcos Ancelovici's Canada Research Chair in the Sociology of Social Conflicts for financial support. Finally, we are grateful to Juan Luis Sotillo for allowing us to use his picture of a Madrid autonomous squat for the cover of the book and to Dimitri Roussopoulos for welcoming this book at Black Rose Books.

Introduction
Subverting Politics with George Katsiaficas

Marcos Ancelovici
Université du Québec à Montréal (UQAM), Canada

This book celebrates the twenty-fifth anniversary of the publication of George Katsiaficas' classic *The Subversion of Politics: European Autonomous Social Movements and the Decolonization of Everyday Life* (2006 [1997]).[1] Among the hundreds of books that discuss social movements, why celebrate Katsiaficas' 25 years after its publication? First of all, when it came out in 1997, *The Subversion of Politics* was the first book to draw a comprehensive picture of autonomous social movements in several European countries.[2] In addition to surveying workerist Italian *Autonomia* and analyzing the exemplary West German Autonomen, it also presented the state of autonomous mobilizations in Amsterdam (The Netherlands) and Copenhagen (Denmark), putting them in the context of the crisis of Fordism and capitalism as well as in that of the Cold War.[3]

Furthermore, it discussed at length the centrality of squats as free spaces and acknowledged the growing influence of feminism in urban social movements. With such scope and richness, Katsiaficas significantly contributed to making autonomous movements visible in intellectual and academic debates. This was no minor feat. Indeed, the West German Greens—which had emerged after autonomous movements in the late 1970s—grabbed most of the attention at the time, and other radical or left-libertarian movements tended to be presented as part of the Greens. As a result, the German Autonomen were either ignored or seen as irrelevant (Katsiaficas 2006 [1997]: 10). In this respect, in his book Katsiaficas shares a telling anecdote:

> In 1989, after I made a detailed presentation at MIT to several hundred people on the Autonomen, which included slides and copies of their magazines, one member of the audience confronted me with the charge that I had invented the whole movement, contending that the events I had described were simply part of the Greens. (2006 [1997]: 10)

Another reason for wanting to celebrate the twenty-fifth anniversary of the book was its engagement with theoretical debates and towering figures of contemporary critical thinking such as Toni Negri, Michael Hardt, and Jürgen Habermas. After discarding Negri and Hardt's work on grounds that it suffered from a "rejection of dialectical thinking, [a] fetishization of production, and a failure to deal with patriarchal domination" (Katsiaficas 2006 [1997]: 217), Katsiaficas substantially engaged with the work of Habermas. He thus built on Habermas' concept of the "colonization of the life-world" (according to which commodification and instrumental rationality are taking over private domains and intimate spheres) to claim that the "decolonization" of everyday life and civil society was the most defining feature of contemporary autonomous social movements. In making such a claim, Katsiaficas was extending the analysis he had started to develop in *The Imagination of the New Left* (1987), in which he surveyed the main radical and revolutionary movements of the late 1960s and 1970s and of which *The Subversion of Politics* was the sequel.

It is worth pointing out that Katsiaficas was engaging with the aforementioned theoretical debates not only on the basis of his reading of theoretical works, including those of his former professor Herbert Marcuse, but also and perhaps more importantly on the basis of his own participation in the German Autonomen. He lived in Berlin from 1979 to 1981, and visited again in 1988, 1991, and 1993, and each time he stayed in a collective house in the (at the time) working-class neighborhood of Kreuzberg (Katsiaficas 2006 [1997]: xvi). He thus wrote his book from inside the movement or from an insider's perspective. Such a combination of theoretical engagement and ambition at the crossroads of activism and qualitative sociology is relatively rare in the study of social movements. It is perhaps the reason why *The Subversion of Politics* was co-winner of the 1998 Michael

Harrington Award of the New Political Science section of the American Political Science Association.

Finally, we thought it was worth celebrating Katsiaficas's book because of its relevance and timeliness in a decade—the 2010s—that witnessed the resurgence or emergence of autonomy-inspired movements in many countries across Europe, North America, and Latin America. From the Indignados and Occupy to Antifa, from Indigenous mobilizations at Standing Rock to Black Lives Matter, from radical feminists to climate justice activists, the influence of the ideals and practices of autonomy seemed more alive and pervasive than ever.

What is Autonomy?

Although the understanding and meaning of autonomy vary depending on the period, country, and demographic segment, it is possible to identify common traits that are present in the manifold autonomous movements that have come and gone since the 1970s. For example, in her account of the emergence of the 15-M (aka the Indignados) in Spain, Flesher Fominaya (2020: 45-46) stresses their horizontal networks, self-organization, direct democracy, direct action, and independence from political parties and trade unions. She identifies several features that apply to most, if not all, autonomous movements. These include prefigurative practices that anticipate the ideal society to which activists aspire; a heterogeneous and often not explicit ideological base; "a rejection of assistentialism, clientelism, and charity models;" and "a DIY (do it yourself) philosophy" (Flesher Fominaya 2020: 46-47).

In addition to these features, Katsiaficas emphasizes the fact that autonomous movements favor a particular relation to power and the state. He explains that:

> Unlike other movements of the twentieth century that have been preoccupied with seizing national power, [autonomous movements] seek to dissolve it... They do not seek to create mammoth structures of power, nor are they interested in participating in existing ones... Autonomous movements have been called "postpolitical" because of their lack of regard for elections and political parties. I prefer to think of these movements as subverting politics, as transforming political participation into something completely different

from what is commonly understood as political. (Katsiaficas 2006 [1997]: 6)

To some extent, these principles were shared by several social movements of the 1960s and there is thus some continuity between the social movements of the 1960s and those of the 1980s (Katsiaficas 2006 [1997]: 3-4). However, Katsiaficas points out that autonomous movements started to use the label "autonomous" to distinguish themselves from Marxist-Leninist groups that not only envisioned change primarily through the seizure of state power but also "denied the value of spontaneous forms of militant resistance" (Katsiaficas 2006 [1997]: 8).[4]

Despite the aforementioned elements of continuity, Katsiaficas argued that many activists of the 1980s thought that the previous generation was not radical enough and had been co-opted by the system. Furthermore, he stated that "more than anything else, the new radicals [of the 1980s] are distinguished from the New Left by their orientation to themselves—to a 'politics of the first person'—not to the proletariat or the wretched of the earth" (Katsiaficas 2006 [1997]: 4). This "politics of the first person" is a defining feature of autonomous movements. It implies that activists cannot claim to speak in the name of a collective, a given social category (e.g., African Americans, women, LGBTQ individuals, etc.), or a mythical figure of revolutionary politics like the "people" or the "working class." Activists can only speak in their own name and must take responsibility for their stances and actions. It is, therefore, a complete rejection of the principles of delegation and representation that lie at the heart of modern politics and, at a practical level, it entails that even having a spokesperson could be an issue. As the very first thesis of the 1981 "Autonomous Theses" puts it:

> We do not engage in "representative struggles." Our activities are based on our own affectedness, "politics of the first person." We do not fight for ideology, or for the proletariat, or for the "people." We fight for a self-determined life in all aspects of our existence, knowing that we can only be free if we are all free. ("Autonomous Theses 1981," in Geronimo 2012 [1990]: 173.)[5]

According to Katsiaficas (2006 [1997]: 15), this new politics is intertwined with the material conditions of late capitalism and the erosion of the traditional bases of leftwing politics. It is also reflected in the autonomous movements' politicization of everyday life as a site of struggle. He explains:

> Rather than pursue careers and create patriarchal families, participants in autonomous movements live in groups to negate the isolation of individuals imposed by consumerism. They seek to decolonize everyday life. The base of the autonomous movement in dozens of squatted and formerly squatted houses reflects a break with the established norms of middle-class propriety in their everyday lives: communes instead of traditional families; movements restaurants and bars where the "scene" can have its own spaces, as opposed to the commercialized world of mass culture; an international community defined by its radical actions, in contrast to the patriotic spectacles so beloved in Europe. (Katsiaficas 2006 [1997]: 6)

Autonomous movements are thus not only political but also (counter)cultural and involve a particular lifestyle. They build on, and foster, urban alternative subcultures that challenge dominant norms. They prioritize the development of free spaces such as squats and social centers, and they cultivate a sense of belonging to the movement as a community.[6] Communal life is a central aspect of this dynamic insofar as it contributes to providing the material and relational conditions to the decolonization of everyday life. Without this communal dimension, we may wonder to what extent a social movement, in which activists essentially meet in public spaces and return to their individual homes at night, can develop the relational dynamics that Katsiaficas presents as characteristics of autonomy.

The Boundaries of Autonomy

Although Katsiaficas argues that autonomous movements "define the phenomenal form of contemporary radical activism," his portrayal of autonomy, as he acknowledges himself, is historically and culturally situated (2006 [1997]: 9). He chose to focus on Italy, Germany, the Netherlands, and Denmark primarily because he already had close ties with activists in those countries and was involved in the movement in Berlin.

Simultaneously, he discarded several other European countries on the belief that the radical politics there was not truly autonomous. For example, he decided not to include Spain and Portugal in his book because he thought that in these countries, social movements "were not oriented toward the transformation of everyday life" (Katsiaficas 2006 [1997]: 8). Similarly, he ruled out France on the grounds that almost all social movement activity there takes place "within the realm of established politics... Creating contested domains outside arenas normally regarded as political is practically inconceivable there" (Katsiaficas 2006 [1997]: 9).[7] Had Katsiaficas considered these countries, he would have probably proposed a slightly different analysis of autonomy.[8] He was thus confronted with the challenge of determining the right level of abstraction, between, on the one hand, idiosyncratic descriptions that yield no epistemic gain and, on the other hand, very thin and abstract conceptualizations that can apply to so many cases that they become irrelevant (for a discussion, see Ancelovici 2021: 127).

The conceptualization of autonomy matters if we want to identify and trace (dis)continuities across time and space. When and where does autonomy cease to be autonomy? First, autonomy varies across time. In this respect, it is worth pointing out a few differences between Italian and German autonomy. Italian autonomous movements focused on class struggle. They employed a workerist discourse, were associated with several famous intellectuals and theoretical works, and engaged in armed struggle. German autonomous movements focused on the decolonization of everyday life, relied on a politics of the first person, were significantly influenced by feminism, but, simultaneously, were not really associated with any particular author or theory.[9] They engaged in punctual and restrained forms of violence such as the Black Bloc tactic,[10] and called for the destruction of private property in the context of confrontations with the police. The point is not that one form of autonomy is more genuine than the other, but rather that the concrete form that autonomy takes is dependent on both internal dynamics and the socio-economic, political, and cultural context wherein these dynamics unfold (cf. Ancelovici 2021). For example, the context of the 1980s and 1990s, characterized by post-Fordism, the rise of new urban middle classes, and the end of the Cold War, is significantly different from that of the

1960s and 1970s. Similarly, the context of the 2010s and 2020s, with hyper-gentrification, the global rise of populism and the far right, and the massification of new information and communication technologies, differs from the 1990s and we can assume that autonomy is no longer what is used to be. As Katsiaficas explains:

> The movements I describe and analyze here are specific to the political and cultural conditions that formed certain European countries' action-possibilities in a specific period of time. The conditions in these countries have already changed—as have their movements. Nowhere do they exist today as I have portrayed them in this book. (2006 [1997]: x)

My point here is not simply that autonomy is neither universal nor ahistorical. It is that even with relatively clear criteria and indicators, tracing a line in the sand and identifying the boundaries of autonomy can be a challenging task. For example, direct democracy and assemblies are often mentioned as a defining feature of autonomous movements (e.g., Flesher Fominaya 2020). However, one could argue that today such practices are at the core of most social movements and thus not specific to autonomy. Furthermore, the status of assemblies can vary or be contested. According to Leach (2013: 188), among West German Autonomen, decisions were often made in affinity groups rather than full assemblies. Similarly, in more recent social movements inspired by autonomy, such as the Indignados and Occupy, the relevance and legitimacy of assemblies were often questioned on grounds that they can foster homogenization as well as new forms of hierarchy and domination. According to anarchist activists participating in the 2011 occupation of Plaça de Catalunya, in downtown Barcelona:

> The beautiful thing about the encampment in the plaza was that it had multiple centers for creation and initiative-taking. The central assembly functioned to suppress this. ... The central assembly did not give rise to one single initiative. What it did, rather, was to grant legitimacy to initiatives worked out in the commissions; but this process must not be portrayed in positive terms. This granting of legitimacy was in fact a robbing of the legitimacy of all the decisions made in the multiple spaces throughout the plaza not incorporated into an official commission. (Anonymous, 2012: 24-25.)[11]

7

Although autonomy and anarchy partly overlap rather than being synonymous, as I pointed out earlier (see note 4), the above quote shows that assemblies are an object of struggle in and of themselves and that we cannot treat their presence in a movement as an objective indicator of autonomy. An emphasis on the decolonization of everyday life and the use of a politics of the first person would perhaps be more relevant criteria, as Katsiaficas argues, but grey zones and ambiguities inevitably remain, and the boundaries of autonomy are always a fleeting reality.

The challenge of identifying the boundaries of autonomy arises as well when we consider the trajectories of cohorts of activists. For example, when leftwing coalitions won the municipal election in Barcelona and Madrid in 2015, many autonomous activists who had been involved in these coalitions took a job in the municipal government and thus entered state institutions (see Ancelovici and Emperador Badimon 2017). On the one hand, insofar as these activists were inside the state, they were no longer, by definition, part of the autonomous movement. It is partly for such reason that the German Autonomen rejected the Greens in the 1980s (see Katsiaficas 2006 [1997]: 196-209). On the other hand, however, these activists inside municipal institutions supported autonomous spaces like squats, often denounced the repression targeting autonomous movements, and tried to promote cultural and social demands partly associated with these groups. Moreover, while they were inside state institutions, many of these activists continued to participate in autonomous spaces (Ancelovici and Emperador Badimon 2017). Therefore, instead of assuming that these activists are allies at best or adversaries at worst, perhaps our analysis would benefit from treating them as *part* of autonomous movements, in the same way that Banaszak (2010) argues that feminists inside the state are not mere allies but part of the women's movement.

Such a claim may be too provocative or even erroneous, but it has the merit of avoiding a reification and simplification of autonomous movements. It posits that symbolic boundaries are porous and dynamic, and that autonomy is a set of ambiguous principles embodied in diverse social relations and practices that cannot be boiled down to a soundbite or slogan.

It also pinpoints the potential biases of applying labels to individuals and groups from above, regardless of how they perceive themselves.

In the end, the challenge and responsibility of such conceptual and analytical work fall on the person telling the story of the movement. This story is likely to vary depending on that person's social position and relation to the movement. In this respect, the authors in this book all have some experience as activists in several, distinct autonomous movements and their respective contributions were influenced by this experience.

In Chapter 1, Jason Del Gandio proposes a narrative of coming of age to explain how he developed a desire for autonomy. In Chapter 2, AK Thompson discusses the fate of autonomous movements and asks how they might subvert politics today. In Chapter 3, Miguel Martínez presents the importance of squats in autonomous movements in Italy, Germany, and Spain. In Chapter 4, Émeline Fourment looks at debates between leftist activists and feminists in the German Autonomen with respect to the issue of sexual violence. In Chapter 5, Rachel Sarrasin accounts for the dynamics of collective autonomy in the anti-authoritarian community of Montreal, Quebec, since 2000. In Chapter 6, Anna Kruzynski recounts how the mobilization of the Autonomous Social Centre, in the working-class neighborhood of Pointe-Saint-Charles, in Montreal, led to the establishment of Building 7, a self-managed space. Finally, in Chapter 7, Richard Day and Robert Lovelace put autonomy in the (post)colonial context and ask how Settlers and Indigenous peoples can work together for greater autonomy.

These chapters shed light on dimensions and cases that Katsiaficas did not consider, but share with him an in-between position. Indeed, Katsiaficas tells an insider's story, but he is also critical of autonomous movements. He has one foot inside and the other outside, in academia. The interest and legitimacy of his account derive in great part from such an ambivalent relationship.

Nothing prepared young Katsiaficas for such a relationship. Indeed, he paradoxically grew up within the U.S. Army, which was perhaps the exact embodiment of anti-autonomy. As he recalls:

It was not easy for me to participate in the movement. My father was a career military man, a highly decorated war hero, who didn't want to see his "only son throw his life away." He would come to demonstrations and physically try to make me leave. I was twenty years old, a senior at MIT, and had more than physical altercation with him. It was very embarrassing and he sometimes hurt me. Nonetheless I persisted.[12]

And persist, he did. He has spent his life studying and participating in autonomous movements from Germany and the United States to South Korea. Such dedication is a testament to the strength of his convictions and an invitation to follow him along a very fruitful and hopeful path. As he puts it, "My own project begins with a very simple proposition: millions of ordinary people, acting together, can profoundly change the basic facts of social life."[13]

Endnotes

1 I wish to thank Francis Dupuis-Déri for comments and suggestions on an earlier draft of this introduction. I obviously remain solely responsible for the resulting text.

2 Geronimo published his classic *Fire and Flame: A History of the German Autonomist Movement* earlier, in 1990, but it focused exclusively on Germany and did not really engage in theoretical debates.

3 I present below the differences between the Italian and the German strand of autonomy.

4 Some autonomous activists also distinguished themselves from anarchism. As the fourth thesis of the 1981 "Autonomous Theses" states, "We all embrace a 'vague anarchism' but we are not anarchists in a traditional sense." See "Autonomous Theses 1981," in Geronimo (2012 [1990]: 174). The "Autonomous Theses 1981" were neither consensual nor a formal program. Nonetheless, according to Geronimo (2012 [1990]: 173), "to this day the straightforward convictions and sentiments listed in the original paper remain at the core of autonomous identity, even if every single one of them has been passionately discussed and, at times, decidedly rejected by parts of the movement."

5 However, some authors question this insistence on the "politics of the first person." For instance, in his chapter in this book, Miguel A. Martínez states: "Although most authors mention this individualistic feature to distinguish autonomism from the more authoritarian, hierarchical, and bureaucratic organizations of the institutional left, I do not find this view very informative. ... More than a tension between the individual and the social dimensions present in all social phenomena, I argue that it is the specific emphasis given to the political method of autonomism (self-or-

ganization and self-management, autonomy from capitalism, patriarchy and racism) and their immediatist engagement in various contentious campaigns that makes it distinct compared to other political identities."

6 For a broader argument about social movements as communities rather than just series of protest events, see Staggenborg (1998).

7 It would be interesting to see how Katsiaficas would make sense of the several *Zones à défendre* (ZAD), meaning literally "zones to defend," that regularly spring up here and there in France to protect certain territories from state intervention. In the 2010s, one ZAD got significant public visibility in Western France, close to Nantes, as it was squatted on for several years in an effort to oppose the construction of a new airport and build an alternative micro-society (activists eventually managed to stop the airport project).

8 For a broad analysis of European autonomous movements that also takes into account Spain, the United Kingdom, Poland, and Austria, see van der Steen et al (2014). For a closer look at autonomy in Spain in the 1970s, see Anonymous (2018 [2008]).

9 I am not arguing that feminism was not present in Italian *Autonomia* in the 1970s, but rather that it was not seen as a central tenet. The cult of the working class and workerist discourse dominated Italian radical politics, to the extent that many feminists active in radical groups like *Lotta Continua* (Struggle Continues) left on grounds that the group was not taking women's issues—such as abortion, sexual violence, or reproductive work—seriously. As a result, the Italian women's movement radicalized and became increasingly autonomous not only from parties and unions, but also from men and male organizations. Eventually, feminism became one of the main currents of Italian radical politics and *Autonomia*. According to Katsiaficas, "In many of the most significant dimensions of the meaning of autonomy, feminist currents were the most significant single source of modern autonomous movements" (2006 [1997]: 35). However, it would take a while for feminist movements to be recognized as central to autonomy. It is because such recognition was more apparent in Germany than Italy that I treat the status of feminism as a feature that distinguishes German autonomy from the Italian variety.

10 On the emergence and practice of the Black Bloc tactic, see Dupuis-Déri (2014).

11 For a discussion of this issue in Occupy Montreal, see Ancelovici (2016).

12 George Katsiaficas, "The Intersection of Biography and History," retrieved from https://www.eroseffect.com/biography on June 28, 2021.

13 Idem.

References

Ancelovici, Marcos. 2016. "Occupy Montreal and the Politics of Horizontalism." Pp. 175-201 in *Street Politics in the Age of Austerity: From the Indignados to Occupy*, edited by Marcos Ancelovici, Pascale Dufour, and Héloïse Nez. Amsterdam: Amsterdam University Press.

Ancelovici, Marcos. 2021. "Conceptualizing the Context of Collective Action: An Introduction." *Social Movement Studies* 20(2):125-38.

Ancelovici, Marcos, and Montserrat Emperador Badimon. 2017. "Espoirs et réalités du municipalisme espagnol. Entretien avec Pablo Carmona." *Revue Contretemps*. Available online here: https://www.contretemps.eu/municipalisme-madrid-carmona/

Anonymous. 2012. "The Characteristics of the Occupation (Barcelona)." Pp. 22-38 in *Occupy Everything: Anarchists in the Occupy Movement, 2009-2011*, edited by Aragorn! Berkeley, CA: LBC Books.

Anonymous. 2018 [2008]. *Le pari de l'autonomie: Récits de luttes dans l'Espagne des années 70*. Paris, France: Éditions du Soufflet.

Banaszak, Lee Ann. 2010. *The Women's Movement Inside and Outside the State*. New York, NY: Cambridge University Press.

Dupuis-Déri, Francis. 2014. *Who's Afraid of the Black Blocs? Anarchy in Action Around the World*. Oakland, CA: PM Press.

Flesher Fominaya, Cristina. 2020. *Democracy Reloaded: Inside Spain's Political Laboratory from 15-M to Podemos*, New York, NY: Oxford University Press.

Geronimo. 2012 [1990]. *Fire and Flame: A History of the German Autonomist Movement*. Oakland, CA: PM Press.

Katsiaficas, George. 2001. "The Necessity of Autonomy," *New Political Science*, vol. 23 (4): 547-555.

Katsiaficas, George. 2006 [1997]. *The Subversion of Politics: European Autonomous Social Movements and the Decolonization of Everyday Life*. Oakland, CA: AK Press.

Leach, Darcy K. 2013. "Culture and the Structure of Tyrannylessness." *The Sociological Quarterly* 54(2):159–228.

Staggenborg, Suzanne. 1998. "Social Movement Communities and Cycles of Protest: The Emergence and Maintenance of a Local Women's Movement." *Social Problems* 45(2):180–204.

van der Steen, Bart, Ask Katzeff, and van Hoogenhuijze (Eds.). 2014. *The City Is Ours: Squatting and Autonomous Movements in Europe from the 1970s to the Present*. Oakland, CA: PM Press.

Chapter 1

The Desire for Autonomy
A Personal Narrative, of Sorts

Jason Del Gandio
Temple University, United States

"The goal of autonomous social movements is the subversion of politics: the decolonization of everyday life...not the conquest of state power." (Katsiaficas 2006: 267)

"Desire produces reality, or stated another way, desiring-production is one and the same thing as social production." (Deleuze & Guattari 2009: 30)

"This essay employs psychological categories because they have become political categories." (Marcuse 1966: xxvii)

There are numerous reasons why people come to desire alternative social orders that oppose hierarchical relations, state control, and centralized governing structures. This essay uses my own personal narrative to investigate the constitution of such a desire. The hope is that focusing on my own experience provokes a larger discussion about related issues. Some questions that I am exploring include: Why do people desire autonomy? Does that desire simply follow from a logical investigation of capitalism and the nation-state or do psychological, emotional, and/or existential factors play a role? What is the relationship between one's personal experience and one's longing for and commitment to an alternative world? What role might trauma play in the construction of autonomous desire? Do present day social structures produce collective trauma, and if so, how might we speak to that collective trauma in ways that mobilize collective autonomous action?

An Early Vision

My adolescent years were uneventful, revolving around sports, minor mischief, and high school anxieties common to a lower middle-class kid. Then, in my late teens, I was fortunate to experience various subcultural scenes—raves, house parties, jam bands, backyard concerts, underground music, afterhours clubs, and other alternative affairs. Living in northern New Jersey 25 miles south of New York City allowed for wonderful indiscretions, many of which were fueled by mind-expanding adventures and a longing for existential meaning and purpose.

Within a short time, I went from suburban jock to disaffected ruffneck counterculturalist. By age 20 I began to see the United States of America as superficial, materialistic, and spiritually vacuous, and I openly talked about the need for revolution. I longed for a decentered, autonomous way of life that would allow each of us to pursue our true selves. I wanted a society that would be celebratory, expressive, mutually supportive, exploratory, and nomadic. Our "movement" wouldn't necessarily involve physical travel, but rather, engender an openness to new ideas, experiences, relations, visions, and ways of being. Even the old could be new and we would caution against the new becoming old and reified. There would be no norms to follow since everyday life would be improvisational—a collective spontaneous dance in which we freely borrow from and advance one another's subjectivities. This open form of life wouldn't revolve around jobs, school, careers, or even family, but around our creative potentials and the rhythms and flows of our natural connections with each other. Such a collective subjectivity would, by necessity, undermine the very possibility of the present social system and thus provoke a full-blown revolution. I was not yet familiar with the life and works of famed 1960s counterculturalist Abbie Hoffman, but his words aptly summarize my own vision. He imagines:

> ...a nation of alienated young people. We carry it around with us as a state of mind in the same way the Sioux Indians carried the Sioux Nation around with them. It is a nation dedicated to cooperation versus competition, to the idea that people should have better means of exchange than property or money, that there should be some other basis for human interaction. (Levine, McNamee, & Greenberg 1970: 140-141)

An inspiring vision, but its politics are complicated. My middle-class education never covered social movements, collective resistance, or the state's use of violence to maintain power. Additionally, my privileged location in the world—as a white, straight, North American, cisgendered male—shielded me from many of the oppressions and inequalities experienced by others. Dropping out of society and creating an alternative culture *is* a viable political option. However, it is a difficult vision to enact when millions of people are struggling to feed, clothe, and house themselves. It is also difficult to argue for when millions of people are psychologically attached to the very system you want them to reject. Even if all things were equal and enough people were willing and able to drop out, the current regime of state-power would surely halt a mass exodus. The system needs bodies to maintain itself and mass withdraw jeopardizes its stability. Some kind of political education would also be necessary, and not just in terms of physical rebellion and conflict, but also in the creation of new subjectivities capable of creating a new society. How do we enact a world that we've never experienced? How do we manifest a vision into a reality? How do we enact autonomous desires that have not been crafted or cultivated?

Revolutionary Vibrations

I had already been enrolled in college, but had not taken it seriously and even dropped out at one point. After a series of existential insights and personal changes, I decided to reenroll, majoring in philosophy with a minor in communication studies. I was convinced that ideas change the world and I fully dedicated myself to my studies. Some of my professors took notice and persuaded me to apply to graduate school. I wound up in southern Illinois with a plan to write a doctoral dissertation on the human vibe, or what I would come to refer to as "bodily emanation"—the transmission of energy between human bodies.[1] There is a clear trajectory between my countercultural experiences and my philosophy of the vibe. Who, without such experiences, would write a 200-page academic treatise on human vibrations?

In April of 2000, I attended an academic conference in Detroit, Michigan. It was my first-ever conference presentation—on the vibe, no less. After presenting my paper and anxiously networking with some folks in the field, I headed to my hotel room to relax.

The evening news was covering protests down in Washington, DC, and that's when the trajectory of my life suddenly changed. Tens of thousands of people were marching in the streets, challenging the engines of corporate globalization. I knew nothing about the politics of the global justice movement.[2] But for some reason I immediately identified with the protesters and their actions. The World Bank and International Monetary Fund were the targets of the day, but these institutions merely symbolized the larger system of neoliberal economics in which traditional democratic institutions and structures—like government, education, mass media, and healthcare—become extensions of market activity with the sole purpose of increasing private wealth. As I would soon learn, billions of people live on less than $2.00 a day; CEOs earn three-hundred times that of average workers; most goods and products are made overseas in abusive, inhumane sweatshops; politicians are bought and sold by the biggest donors; and corporations can sue national governments for passing laws that hinder profit even when those laws benefit citizens. It's barbaric and disgusting.

My political awakening also attuned me to my immediate situation. People were flooding the streets and placing their bodies on the line while I was tucked away in a million-dollar conference center. They were yelling and marching while I was presenting and networking. They were staring down riot cops while I was ignoring the realities of Detroit—a deindustrialized, Black-majority city that in years to come would epitomize the ravages of the neoliberal economic order.

My unexpected radical awakening can be explained, in part, by George Katsiaficas' (1987) concept of the "eros effect." He explains that:

> Such spontaneous leaps may be, in part, a product of long-term social processes in which organized groups and conscious individuals prepare the groundwork, but when political struggle comes to involve millions of people, it is possible to glimpse a rare historical occurrence: the emergence of the *eros* effect, the massive awakening of the in-

stinctual human need for justice and freedom. When the *eros* effect occurs, it becomes clear that the fabric of the *status quo* has been torn, and the forms of social control have been ruptured. (Katsiaficas 1987: 10, all emphasis in the original)

I was not yet part of the "millions" described by Katsiaficas, but I intuitively understood, in a pre-rational, desirous manner, the impetus for large-scale radical action. But ironically, I was *not* moved in the same way by the historic "Battle in Seattle" which had occurred just a few months prior. Fifty-thousand people shutting down the World Trade Organization had put the global justice movement on the map. I had caught some of the coverage in much the same way as the DC protests. But I was unaffected. This may seem strange, but awakenings and desires are not constituted through one-to-one causal relationships. Subliminal processes do not move along linear chains of computation; they don't move sequentially and additionally. It's not point A-*plus*-point B-*equals*-point C. Instead, they follow their own nonlinear progressions, jumping and oscillating from K to E to * to _____. That blank represents the open-ended unpredictability of subconscious desire, and such desire follows a logic of its own.[3] As the Invisible Committee (2009) argues:

Revolutionary movements do not spread by contamination but by resonance. Something that is constituted here resonates with the shock wave emitted by something constituted over there. A body that resonates does so according to its own mode. An insurrection is not like a plague or a forest fire—a linear process which spreads from place to place after an initial spark. It rather takes the shape of a music, whose focal points, though dispersed in time and space, succeed in imposing the rhythms of their own vibrations, always taking on more density. (Invisible Committee 2009: 12-13)

My desire for political rebellion was triggered by the vibrations of global justice, and ever since that day in Detroit I've committed my life to radical social change. I picked up the hotel's free copy of *USA Today* and looked for stories about these protests. I returned to southern Illinois and checked out books from the library. I raised discussions among my friends and debated family members. I looked for protests to attend and began plugging in to this "movement of movements."

An Intellectual Milieu

Spontaneous political awakenings may appear to erupt out of nowhere, but precipitating factors always play a role. The global justice movement had been happening a few years prior to Seattle. Likewise, the Arab Spring was a response to decades of theocratic dictatorships; Occupy Wall Street occurred amid the Great Recession and ever-increasing economic inequality; and Black Lives Matter can be understood as the most recent iteration of a Black freedom movement dedicated to ending White supremacy.

Similar insights apply to *personal* transformation. Every individual has a preceding history and exists within a wider environment of influence. My countercultural experiences prepared the soil for my awakening while my graduate studies provided an environment to grow my thoughts and ideas.

For graduate school, I was in a department of communication studies, focusing on the philosophy of communication and performance studies. For me, that meant studying how human beings create their realities through our communicative interaction. My department was community-oriented and encouraged us to discuss and apply what we were learning. My cohort of friends often talked over pints of beers during happy hour or at late-night weekend parties. (Contrary to what some may think, grad-students can definitely party. In our case, it was a necessity born from the rigors of grad-school and another form of intellectual collaboration.) Some of the major topics of discussion included the constitution of subjectivity, the performance of everyday life, the analysis of popular discourse, and the communicative dimensions of power-relations, all with an emphasis on identity politics and the discursivity of the body. And while the term "intersectionality" was not yet common, we regularly discussed standpoints, locations, and positionalities. The study of these topics was informed by our reading of Edmund Husserl, Martin Heidegger, Maurice Merleau-Ponty, Jacques Derrida, Michel Foucault, Jean-François Lyotard, Judith Butler, Paulo Freire, bell hooks, and many others. We also studied the radical performance art of Joseph Beuys, Karen Finley, Carolee Schneemann, Hermann Nitsch, Marina Abramovic, Allan

Kaprow, and Richard Foreman, and debated the merits of auto-ethnography and autobiographical performance.

In the fall of 1999, I took my second course on communication and gender. This particular class had a profound impact on my development, enabling me to understand how each of us is situated within a communicatively-constituted matrix of social stratification. Some identities are valorized while others oppressed, some elevated while others marginalized, some privileged while others silenced. I shockingly realized that I was not outside of this social configuration. My white, male, heterosexual body perpetuated the very oppressions I opposed. More dreadfully still was the fact that I inherited these conditions. The world is already in motion when we are born and we are forced to adopt the customs and habits of our surrounding society. As Heidegger (1996) might say, we are thrown into a world not of our own making.

These unacceptable realities ignited an inner rage: How could I ever resist let alone overturn *an entire world* that I opposed? The human condition appeared brutal and unforgiving. These insights also brought to light my own emotional struggles. I had been holding on to unresolved childhood trauma and ignoring feelings of fear, resentment, and inadequacy. Throughout my life I had convinced myself that bad things happen to good people every day. It's no big deal, I thought. I don't need anyone's sympathy and I don't want anyone's help. But this class forced me to examine the intricacies of human subjectivity. I soon learned that my own everyday performance of white-straight-cis gendered-hypermasculinity was in effect a self-defense mechanism, shielding me from my own trauma. As bell hooks argues, "patriarchy benefits no one" (hooks 2000: ix).

Although men occupy a position of privilege, that privilege comes with costs that infect all levels of society. There really is no way to dislodge the personal from the political. How I exist in the world inherently affects others. I wasn't quite ready to handle these newly-surfaced emotions, but I did realize that creating a better world involves working on oneself. Grappling with my unresolved emotions—and their connections to my inherited privilege and power—is a lifelong process. But I began there in that graduate course and it prepared me for the radical awakening that was to come just a few months later in Detroit.

I must note, however, that working on oneself does not necessarily lead to radical transformation. If it did, then the billion-dollar therapy industry would have already revolutionized the world. Self-work must be coupled with other kinds of work—*political work*. To again quote hooks:

> If one's identity is constructed from a base of power and privilege gained from participation in and acceptance of structures of domination, it is not a given that focus on naming that identity will lead to radicalized consciousness, a questioning of that privilege, or to active resistance. It is possible to name one's personal experience without committing oneself to transforming or changing that experience. (hooks 1989: 108)

> It is only as allies with those who are exploited and oppressed, working in struggles for liberation, that individuals who are not victimized demonstrate their allegiance, their political commitment, their determination to resist, to break with the structure of domination that offer them personal privilege. This holds true for individuals from oppressed and exploited groups as well. Our consciousness can be radicalized by acting to eradicate forms of domination that do not have direct correspondence with our identities and experiences. (hooks 1989: 109)

Direct Action and Mass Arrest

It's September 2002, and I am a newly minted Ph.D. I am living in New York City and beginning my first full time faculty position at Hofstra University. By this time, I had become familiar with the trials and tribulations of globalization, attended my fair share of protests, and taken up minor activist activities. The post-September 11th global justice movement was beginning to wane, but it was still six months before America's invasion and occupation of Iraq and the movement and its summit protests were still occurring.

I decided to attend the anti-IMF/World Bank demonstrations that were to occur, again, in DC. The event was dubbed "The People's Strike" and organized, at least in part, by the DC Anti-Capitalist Convergence. On my journey down there, I unwittingly found myself amidst self-defined anarchists and Black Bloc participants preparing for direct action and police confrontations. This was not necessarily shocking to me given the experience and knowledge I had acquired by this time. However, much of that was gleaned from a distance. My graduate studies had taken precedence and my protest activities had been tepid. This time, however, I would be directly participating.

Organizers planned "S27" as a day of mass direct action, which would include, among other things, locking down buildings, clogging intersections, stopping traffic, dropping banners, monkey-wrenching subway token machines, performing street theater, and posting "out of order signs" to confuse pedestrians. The point was to shut down the city and make the meetings impossible. I decided to join a "snake march" that would be weaving its way in and out of downtown streets in the hopes of attracting police attention and enabling others to engage in more militant tactical activity.

But this was not Seattle. City officials had over 3,000 police on hand—about 1,500 from DC and about 1,700 from other jurisdictions from across the country. Cops were stationed on every corner, many of them in riot gear.

It was not overly warm for September, but the overcast and humidity made for a close atmosphere. A low-lying steam emanated from the asphalt while a slight rain penetrated the lingering fog. Morning rush-hour traffic was noticeably light. The sidewalks and subways were unsettlingly clear of pedestrian commuters. Throngs of cops decked in rain gear and clutching nightsticks punctuated the scene.

I don't remember how it started, but by mid-morning the city felt like a war zone. Pepper spray, tear gas, and percussion hand grenades were used, and rubber bullet ammunition was on hand, though I am personally unsure if a trigger was ever pulled.

The snake march was successful, but short lived. One too many skirmishes with police produced an emergent, schizophrenic swarm logic. Protesters and police would clash, and people would scatter in every direction. Then, seemingly out of nowhere, we would spontaneously link back up to hold a corner or block. We would then disperse again when another confrontation became too hot. This link-clash-and-disperse scenario repeated across several city blocks. At one point, about a hundred of us were cornered, pushed up against a ten-foot panoramic bank window. I was somewhere in the middle of the pack, while those in the rear were smashed against the window. The force of bodies splintered the glass and three-foot sheets began crashing down. We miraculously pushed our way out before anyone was seriously injured or killed.

We scattered across more city blocks until a good handful of us became trapped in a small grassy park just a short distance from the White House. The cops outlined the perimeter with bicycles, motorcycles, and Metro buses. Small pockets of people debated what to do. At least one group suggested fighting our way out, but the cops eventually moved in, squeezing us tighter and tighter. We were arrested in plastic handcuffs, placed on to the buses, and driven to various detention centers. Approximately 650 of us were rounded-up over the course of the day. The official charge on my release papers was "failure to obey."

Micro-Fascism

Up until this experience, I still had some faint hope in America's democratic structures—the right to vote, civil liberties, political representation, and a rational, semi-equitable system. But the riot and mass arrest changed that. I learned, firsthand, that state forces can, at any point in time and with little rhyme or reason, revoke my rights and freedoms. Yes, there are laws and bureaucratic checks and balances supposedly safeguarding individual liberties. But a dark reality undergirds it all—a "becoming-fascism," if you will.[4] I openly acknowledge the very real differences between something like Nazi Germany and the United States of America. A truly fascist state may have killed us on the spot. But the dividing line between fascism and representative democracy is not as clear as some may think. Tyranny lurks in the cracks, and a "state of exception" can be invoked at will.

My comments may seem hyperbolic, but "American democracy" is riddled with atrocities: the genocide of indigenousness peoples; the enslavement of Africans; Japanese internment camps; the prison-industrial complex; Guantanamo Bay; the invasion and occupation of sovereign nations; the #NoDAPL standoff; the denial of civil rights to any number of groups;

anti-sodomy laws; electroshock and conversion "therapies;" the murder of African Americans at the hands of police; Immigration and Customs Enforcement agents (ICE) conducting 6am raids on peaceful, law-abiding families; women's bodies scrutinized in the media and controlled by elected representatives; the economic imprisonment of the homeless, hungry, and working poor; the destruction and domination of the natural environment and nonhuman life; and the continued normalization of "white supremacist capitalist patriarchy" (hooks 2000: 5).

In my particular case, I was shipped to the outskirts of the city—out of sight, out of mind. And it is here that my orientation to society changed. Metro buses became cargo vans. A police academy became a detention center. A gymnasium became a gen-pop holding cell. Wrestling matts became prison beds, and democracy became micro-fascism. My right wrist was hog-tied to my left ankle for approximately 26 hours while police officers, sworn to protect and serve, declared, several times, "you are under arrest, you have no rights." The FBI was also on hand creating intelligence files on every arrestee. We were treated as enemies of the state, and upon reflection, they were right.[5]

I acknowledge again that a truly fascist state would have either whisked us away or shot us on sight. But these more extreme possibilities do not mute the undemocratic nature of the modern nation-state: State-power channels individual freedom toward the empowerment of an exterior, alienating "Other." This Other grants us permission to move and resist, but only within very limited restrictions. Even one's resistance is championed as a hallmark of the system's benevolence and righteousness. As the First Amendment to the U.S. Constitution states, the people have the right to peaceably assemble and to petition the government for a redress of grievances. Such a "system of rights" is far better than an outright dictatorship. But the system is still tyrannical by nature, for you are always one down and one removed from the locus of power, confined to living a life that serves another.

A Pedagogy of Autonomy

Marching in the streets and defying state-sanctioned police orders was no doubt terrifying. I was bewildered, overtaken by it all. Running past a cop with a rubber bullet gun pointed at my head was no joke. My hands shook and my knees knocked, literally. But the experience was more than a confrontation with state-power. It was also a *pedagogy of autonomy*.

I learned that we are free to challenge the structures of society and force power to bend to *our* demands. Holding such a position for any length of time is difficult given the state's monopoly on violence and physical coercion. But I agree with Hakim Bey (2003) that we can create zones of temporary autonomy that actualize our latent abilities. For me, this actualization of autonomy points to an ontological undercurrent unique to all living creatures—a decolonized zero-point of orientation that is wanting and able to outmaneuver any and all top-down controls. This "decolonized zero-point of orientation" is similar to an inborn vitalism. There is something unique about the human creature (and perhaps all living creatures) that compels us to overcome impediments to free thought and action. The history of humanity is one of tyranny and control. But it is also one of resistance and rebellion. We find ways to break the barriers no matter the conditions. From this perspective, the human experience is a will-to-autonomy.

My understanding of autonomy is influenced by the Italian autonomist tradition, which argues, in brief, that resistance is primary to human experience.[6] It is commonly assumed that rebellion is a response to oppression, but Italian autonomists argue the opposite: that oppression is a response to rebellion. In other words, the ability to resist comes first, and oppressive systems and structures constantly rearrange themselves to compensate for that resistance. If the opposite were true, then neither resistance nor oppression would be possible, for it is the former that is the dynamic force within human experience. The struggle between these two forces, of which resistance is primary, drives forward the progression of collective experience. In this sense, then, "temporary zones of autonomy" express humanity's primordial rejection of capture and control and our natural inclination toward autonomist desire.[7]

But I must clarify my understanding of "autonomist desire" as both an ontological structure and a psycho-emotional longing. A will-to-autonomy is part and parcel of what we are as human creatures. But any number of obstacles can inhibit our ability to act on that autonomy. That inhibition then produces a psychological longing—a longing to close the gap between this world of capture and control and our ontological nature of openness and freedom. That psychological longing may be ignored or repressed due to social conditioning or outright censure—an overarching "No!" as embodied by the top-down structures of family, schooling, capitalism, patriarchy, the nation-state, etc. That longing can also be dysfunctionally channeled (sublimated) into non-autonomous attitudes and behaviors.

To use a basic example, a child's desire to freely play, connect, and express can be artificially stunted. That desire doesn't simply disappear, but is transformed, perhaps into anger and controlling behaviors. Anger and control can then become habitual gestures carrying over into adulthood and structuring one's daily life. But the primordial desire for play, connection, and expression continues to linger below the surface. And though it is caged and quarantined, that desire periodically reveals itself—at late night drunken parties where everyone is laughing and having fun, during long walks in a quiet forest, or while reading a few inspiring words in a well-written book. These brief moments reveal what we are, deep down, and who we wish to be, all the time. The same is true for our will-to-autonomy: it can show itself in any number of situations, whether on the streets or elsewhere.

Awakening in a Boys' Home

It would be intellectually dishonest of me to end my story here. Yes, there were my countercultural experiences, the intellectualism of graduate school, the Detroit hotel room, and the direct action and mass arrest. But why did these experiences affect me in these specific ways? Surely others had similar experiences that did not lead them on a search for autonomy. What underlies my own propensity for autonomist desire?

Much of my life—and politics—can be traced back to early childhood chaos. Born in 1974, my parents were part of the freewheeling hippie counterculture and enjoyed the excesses of the era. I vividly recall dancing with my parents while cascades of psychedelic tie-die paint shot from a concert stage. But I also recall sitting in a biker bar with people openly trafficking in drugs, guns, and other illegal paraphernalia.

By the time I was five years old my mother had been arrested for selling "downs" to an undercover police officer. Her arrest, which I had witnessed, was the last time I ever saw or spoke to her. Sometime thereafter, my father was also arrested. The details are foggy, but I presume it was for drunk driving, resisting arrest, and assault on a police officer. Sitting in the backseat of our car, in the late hours of the night, I watched him fight the police until he was violently subdued, handcuffed, and hauled away. My world suddenly crumbled, and I can still see the red-and-blue flashes shimmering off the damp humid streets.

I awoke the next morning in a temporary boys' home. Shouts of the other boys jumping from one bunkbed to the next startled me awake. I hid in the crevice between the bunk and wall while peering over the top of a thinly veiled sheet, cautiously observing the action before me. I was never given proper explanation as to why I was there, and I had no language or cognitive framework to understand what I was witnessing. But yet, there it was—a spontaneous melee of young boys reclaiming their humanity and expressing their displeasure with a home that they did not ask for and could not leave. The moment burns eternal in my mind. The boys glowed in the early morning sun—laughing, jumping, rebelling. But alas, I was too terrified to join them, and instead, squeezed myself further against the wall.

One of the home's attendants entered the room to quiet the boys. His voice was firm and authoritative, though not overly harsh. The boys persisted until he smacked a hanger just a few inches from my knees. My instinctive jump-and-gasp caught him off guard as he didn't notice me beneath the sheet. After briefly glancing my way, he turned back to the now silenced boys and corralled us to line up in the hallway.

Many other such details follow from this situation, though those are unimportant for the purposes at hand. Suffice it to say that I was reunited with my father and, eventually, all turned out well. But it was there, in the boy's home, that a cluster of longings began to form—desires to voice my concerns, understand my situation, speak my mind, be heard and appreciated, control my immediate surroundings, participate in collective action, rebel against an inhumane, alienating system, and determine the contours of my own destiny.

Such desires also reflect the rebelliousness of my parents, each of whom experienced their own childhood traumas. They were not politically radical, at least not consciously. There were no marches or demonstrations, no serious engagement with the news or current events, no analysis of capitalism or systemic oppression. But their outlaw lifestyle signified, at least to my young subconscious mind, that I am neither determined by, nor bound to, the wider social framework. A symbiotic relationship between self-and-other always exists, and we never fully eclipse the norms of our society. But we are, ontologically speaking, free to think and act for ourselves.

My father's parenting, though questionable at times, further enforced this belief. When I asked about God, he encouraged me to explore my own ideas. When neighborhood kids pressured me to fight another boy, he told me to think for myself. When I started hanging out in underground scenes, he cautioned me to be smart. These small gestures, on their own, do not produce a desire for autonomy, but they do flesh out a familial environment in which that desire is given room to express itself.

Interpreting Trauma

Despite my own narrative details, it would be a mistake to assume that my adulthood radicalism is a mere manifestation of my childhood trauma. Yes, there is a clear connection and I openly admit that many of my political commitments are firmly rooted in that boys' home experience. But trauma does not arise from the experience itself; instead, it arises from the meaning we assign to experience (Alexander 2012). This is both empowering and frustrating.

It's empowering because the meanings can change and what we once perceived as trauma can become a source of power and inspiration. In my case, the emotional loss of my primary caregivers was equivalent to experiencing their deaths, for there was no way to cognitively grasp their sudden vanishment or possible return. But that experience has also granted me an above-average ability to empathize with the suffering of others. The violence surrounding the loss of my parents produced a general, ever-persistent sense of dread and uncertainty that my psyche subliminally channels into over-controlling behaviors (in technical terms, my psyche is "hyper-vigilant"). But the experience also produced a profound aversion to all unaccountable authoritarian figures and orders. My confinement to the boys' home made me feel emotionally weak, insecure, and insignificant, but it also provided me with a visceral understanding of widespread systemic injustice, which is the source of my radical activist sensibility.

But the ambiguity of meaning is also frustrating because we may not consciously recognize the meanings we are assigning to events/experiences. A one-to-one causal relationship between the experience itself and the meaning we ascribe would be fairly easy to deal with, at least from a therapeutic standpoint: You experienced X, and X means Y; bringing Y to the surface of your conscious mind releases you from the trauma of X. But it's not that simple. The mind produces meanings on top of meanings on top of meanings, all in an effort to hide itself from itself. Neuroses and maladies then arise, making it even more difficult to unravel relations among experiences-and-meanings. It took me over thirty years to come to terms with my childhood. Luckily, my subliminal processes guided me toward "productive" and "healthy" coping mechanisms. But it is safe to assume that not all of the children confined to that boys' home developed along the same lines.

Provoking Autonomous Desire

The telling of my personal story is an act of public catharsis—a therapeutic gesture that enables me to see and understand the "events-and-meanings" of my life. But it's also an attempt to understand the relationship between trauma and the desire for autonomy. If we are in fact autonomist creatures living in a non-autonomist society, then everyday life is perpetually traumatizing. Of course, the ontology that I've outlined here is debatable; any good thinker can substitute one ontology for another and draw different conclusions about what kind of society logically follows. But one can disagree with my philosophical tenets and still agree that modern society produces, and is a product of, *collective* trauma. War, imperialism, colonialism, gross economic inequality, the drudgery of work, mass shootings, mass incarceration, police killings, rape culture, heteronormativity, compulsory-nationalism, and environmental degradation would all seem to produce a collective trauma. Conversely, such behaviors would seem to develop from a traumatized collective. Are we not all young, confused children living out the effects of unresolved traumas?

If the answer is yes, then how might we generate new kinds of meanings that acknowledge and then reroute our shared trauma? How might we devise strategies for channeling our collective trauma toward autonomist ends? How might we model for others decolonized modes of interpretation that evoke nonlinear resonances and awaken autonomist desires? Such therapeutic questioning is not, in and of itself, sufficient for creating revolution. But it seems to be a helpful step in clarifying our wants and needs, sharpening our visions and reality-creating capabilities, and cultivating decolonized subjectivities capable of resisting and eclipsing present day society.

Endnotes

1. For more information on the topic, see Del Gandio (2012). To see how I connect the vibe to spontaneous mass uprisings, see Del Gandio (2014).

2. The movement went by different names—anti-globalization, alter-globalization, counter-globalization, etc. I always preferred the more affirmative expression of global justice.

3. For more on this nonlinear logic, see Del Gandio (2014).

4. Some of my terminology, such as "becoming-fascism" and "schizophrenic," is influenced by the work of Deleuze and Guattari (1987, 2009).

5. For a somewhat related account of arrest-as-pedagogy during "The People's Strike," see Thompson (2010, chapter two). Loadenthal (2002) is also helpful.

6. This line of thought originates with Mario Tronti (1965) and is then taken up and advanced by a variety of thinkers and related traditions. See select passages in Hardt & Virno (1996), Hardt & Negri (2009), Berardi (2009), and Bono & Kemp (1991).

7. This summation is paraphrased from Del Gandio & Thompson (2017: 12).

References

Alexander, J. (2012). *Trauma: A social theory*. Cambridge, UK: Polity Press.

Berardi, F. (2009). *The soul at work: From alienation to autonomy*. Los Angeles, CA: Semiotext(e).

Bey, H. (1991). *TAZ: The temporary autonomous zone, ontological anarchy, and poetic terrorism*. Brooklyn, NY: Autonomedia.

Bono, P. & Kemp, S. (1991). *Italian feminist thought: A reader*. Oxford, UK: Basil Blackwell.

Deleuze, G. & Guattari, F. (1987). *A thousand plateaus: Capitalism and schizo-phrenia* (B. Massumi, Trans). Minneapolis, MN: University of Minnesota Press. (Original work published 1980.)

Deleuze, G. & Guattari, F. (2009). *Anti-oedipus: Capitalism and schizophrenia* (R. Hurley, M. Seem, & H. R. Lane, Trans). New York, NY: Penguin Books. (Original work published 1972.)

Del Gandio, J. (2012). From affectivity to bodily emanation: An introduction to the human vibe. *Phaenex: Journal of Existential and Phenomenological Theory and Culture*, 7(2), 28-58.

Del Gandio, J. (2014). Extending the eros effect: Sentience, reality, and eman-ation. *New Political Science*, 36(2), 129-148. doi: 10.1080/07393148.2014.883799

Del Gandio, J. & Thompson, AK. (Eds.). (2017). *Spontaneous combustion: The eros effect and global revolution*. Albany, NY: SUNY Press.

Hardt, M. & Virno, P. (1996). *Radical thought in Italy: A potential politics*. Min-neapolis, MN: University of Minnesota Press.

Hardt, M. & Negri, A. (2009). *Commonwealth*. Cambridge, MA: Harvard Uni-versity Press.

Heidegger, M. (1996). *Being and time* (J. Stambaugh, Trans.). Albany, NY: SUNY Press. (Original work published 1927.)

hooks, b. (1989). *Talking back: Thinking feminism, thinking black*. Boston, MA: South End Press.

hooks, b. (2000). *Feminism is for everybody: Passionate politics*. Cambridge, MA: South End Press.

Katsiaficas, G. (1987). *The imagination of the new left: A global analysis of 1968*. Boston, MA: South End Press.

Katsiaficas, G. (2006). *The subversion of politics: European autonomous social movements and the decolonization of everyday life*. Oakland, CA: AK Press.

Levin, M. L., McNamee, G. C., & Greenberg, D. (Eds.). (1970). *The tales of Hoff-man*. Toronto, CA: Bantam Books.

Loadenthal, M. (2002). "The People's Strike": Analyzing a day of action by the DC anti-capitalist convergence. Retrieved from https://www.aca-demia.edu/1470318/_2002_The_People_s_Strike_Analyz-ing_A_Day_of_Action_by_the_DC_Anti-Capitalist_Convergence

Marcuse, H. (1966). *Eros and civilization: A philosophical inquiry into Freud*. Bo-ston, MA: Beacon Press. (Original work published 1955.)

The Invisible Committee. (2009). *The coming insurrection*. Los Angeles, CA: Se-miotext(e).

Thompson, AK. (2010). *Black bloc, white riot: Anti-globalization and the genea-logy of dissent*. Oakland, CA: AK Press.

Tronti, M. (1965). The strategy of refusal. Retrieved from http://lib-com.org/library/strategy-refusal-mario-tronti

Chapter 2

The Life and Death of Autonomy:
How Might Politics
Be Subverted Today?

AK Thompson

"The time for our species to seize control of its destiny is rapidly approaching. Let's hope that we are worthy of the task before us."
— George Katsiaficas

I

For more than two decades, and without ever consciously having meant for it to be the case, my political life has been bound to the autonomous tradition and, through it, to the work of George Katsiaficas. Looking back now, it's impossible to ignore the way that Katsiaficas' *Imagination of the New Left* (1987) served as a faithful companion through my years of undergraduate study and struggle.[1] A little later, while I was working on my PhD during the early-mid aughts, Katsiaficas' insights prompted me to help form Autonomy and Solidarity (a short-lived Toronto-based group that drew on autonomous insights to foster the development of radical movement currents). Among other projects, Autonomy and Solidarity gave rise to *Upping the Anti: A Journal of Theory and Action,* a publication that served as my intellectual and political home for the ten issues I spent on its Editorial Committee. Echoing Katsiaficas' call for an autonomous politics that could offer "a revolutionary alternative to both authoritarian socialism ... and 'pseudo-democratic' capitalism,"[2] *Upping the Anti* encouraged its readers and contributors to develop strategies that might escape the impossible choice between "the 'party building' exercises of the sectarian left and the dead-end of social democracy."[3]

In the spring of 2008, *Upping the Anti* published an interview I'd conducted with Katsiaficas to mark the fortieth anniversary of May '68.[4] Shortly thereafter, in 2010, he blurbed a book I'd written ("a manifesto," he called it) about the political significance of black bloc actions during the anti-globalization movement.[5] Still more recently, and prompted by an interesting discussion that took place during the 2013 conference of the International Herbert Marcuse Society in Lexington, Kentucky, I (along with Jason Del Gandio) co-edited a volume dedicated to the elaboration, application, and critical assessment of "the eros effect."[6] This concept, which lies at the heart of Katsiaficas' work, is perhaps his greatest intellectual contribution to the autonomous tradition.

By foregrounding the erotic dimensions of global revolt, Katsiaficas devised a tangible and compelling means of linking diffuse moments of struggle to reveal their affective and strategic continuity. Emphasizing the eros effect, for instance, makes clear that the autonomous insurgencies that arose in Europe during the 1980s were in some ways both a reprise and a logical continuation of the themes and sensibilities that had given the struggles of 1968 their character. But while the eros effect provides additional nuance to the autonomous conception of the "circulation of struggle," it also serves as a critical rejoinder to those anti-humanist and anti-dialectical currents that have become prevalent within autonomous theory.[7] Having first found expression in Italy, these currents are now pervasive throughout the Anglo-American world. In response, and prompted by the need to engage in principled fights with figures like Antonio Negri, Katsiaficas has worked to restore autonomy's dialectical impulse.[8] For this reason (and regardless of where one might stand on the theoretical question), the significance of his contributions has only become more pronounced over time.

Despite the productive intellectual exchanges his work has fostered, however, I only really connected with Katsiaficas' *Subversion of Politics* when AK Press issued a new, revised edition in 2006 (complete with a gracefully redesigned cover, and featuring the sustained engagement with Negri's ideas mentioned above).[9] Looking back on the book now, more than a decade since I first read it and more than two since it was first published, I'm struck by how timely it remains. I'll even confess that it fills me with envy. A suspect emotion, to be sure, but how else is a contemporary US-based radical supposed to respond to Katsiaficas' nonchalant observation that the German Autonomen owed their strength to something other than "overwhelming numbers" when his quantifications stack up like this?

> In June 1987...when President Ronald Reagan visited Berlin, the anonymous "black bloc"...numbered only three thousand of the fifty thousand anti-Reagan demonstrators. And in 1988, when seventy-five thousand protestors gathered at the meeting of the International Monetary Fund and World Bank in Berlin, only a small faction could be counted as Autonomen.[10]

Only! Along with the striking reminder that—even in the Global North—the struggle against corporate globalization (and against targets like the IMF and World Bank) began more than a decade prior to the anti-WTO protests in Seattle, the scale of activity recounted in this passage is difficult to comprehend. And while Katsiaficas may be right that, proportionally speaking, the autonomous forces involved in the Berlin actions were small, this does little to change the fact that—when tactics scale up—they often produce dramatic qualitative transformations in terms of their effects. Moreover, even if we restrict ourselves to a quantitative assessment, "only three thousand" is still nearly ten times greater than the largest black blocs to have ever emerged in the U.S. Since this is the case (and when contemplated from the standpoint of the peril we now face), the mobilizations recounted in *Subversion* are as alluring as they are taunting. Indeed, they are *uncanny*. For even as they seduce with a strange familiarity, their exuberant excess compels us to take a leap off the vertiginous edge. How then, *Subversion* demands, might autonomous movements work to subvert politics today?

II

At its best, and beneath or beyond the envy it provokes, *Subversion* forces us to consider what lessons might be derived from its pages. This is so not least because the recounted events are *historical*; try as we might, we can't return to the time and place that allowed the movement to flourish. Indeed, as Katsiaficas makes clear, the uprisings he describes are inseparable from the "political and cultural conditions that formed certain European countries' action-possibilities in a specific period of time... Nowhere do they exist today as I have portrayed them."[11]

But while such conditions cannot be discounted, placing the emphasis on "action-possibilities" alone can prevent us from coming to terms with the role that the movement itself played in hastening its own demise. In opposition to this tendency, I will here suggest that the movement's fate owed as much to the logical unfolding of contradictions inherent in its conception of autonomy as it did to extrinsic factors.

Through a careful reading of the record of *Subversion*, it becomes clear that this conception enjoined participants to embrace modes of struggle that (regardless of their particular objective) tended to prioritize collapsing the interval between ontology and politics—of making life and the way it's lived the substance of politics as such. And while some means of accomplishing this aim yielded important political gains, others encouraged participants to turn inward and become isolated from their bases of recruitment and support. Nevertheless, because the movement embraced this conception of autonomy in an open-ended fashion, it became possible for participants committed to an array of sometimes-incompatible actions to lay equal claim to the movement's promise and pedigree. Over time, this ecumenical approach tended to favor forms of engagement that were more affirming than consequential, and it was this tendency that assured the movement's demise. To determine how politics might be subverted today, it's necessary to identify the factors that contributed to the conceptual degeneration of the movement's founding principles so that we might avoid a similar outcome.

III

As is often the case with political concepts, defining "autonomy" is no simple task. And in *Subversion*, Katsiaficas even concedes that, superficially, the movement that developed around the concept amounted to little more than a "diffuse collection of militant counterculturalists" who tended to gather and act "sporadically." Consequently, and since its identity was "far from fixed," the movement presented difficulties for anyone trying to pin it down.[12] Despite these challenges, however, the details that Katsiaficas catalogues in *Subversion* provide a telling snapshot.

Recounting how feminist activists elaborated the concept of autonomy during the movement's heyday, Katsiaficas detects a variety of discrete but nested iterations. "On an individual level," he notes, "women were concerned with their personal autonomy." Meanwhile, and from the perspective of the women's *movement*, "autonomy referred to the need for female collective autonomy." Concretely speaking, this meant that participants in movement organizations were committed to fostering "independence within a nonhierarchical framework" and to avoiding "division between leaders and followers." Finally, and from the standpoint of the broader political field, autonomy "referred to the feminist movement's independence from established political parties."[13]

Practically speaking, each of these conceptions enjoined the movement's participants to "live according to a new set of norms" through which "everyday life" might be "transformed." With these improvisational subversions, and especially with respect to those that challenged the limitations of political representation, autonomists sought to politicize the very act of "living" itself. At their threshold, this premise suggested, the new modes of being devised through autonomous experimentation might decolonize "everyday life," thus producing a perfect correspondence between being and doing. By undermining the "hierarchies" that were central to "traditional political relationships," movement participants sought to foster "political interactions in which these roles [were] subverted."[14] And since such roles in turn dictated how life was to be lived, the movement's orientation to subversion made of life both a means and an end. In this way, the normal bourgeois distinction between ontology and politics (between private and public, personal and political) became the target of a direct and multi-faceted attack.

For the bourgeoisie, politics begins with a conception of "man" in the "state of nature." Gifted with natural rights and buoyed by natural law, this man is presumed to be equal to all other men by virtue of the simple fact of his being. Starting from these mystical premises, bourgeois politics aimed to safeguard natural equality while facilitating those interactions that brought men into community with the aim of furthering their individual happiness. In this model, human nature is conceived as being prior to politics, with the latter emerging to organize, cultivate, and protect the former. Movements have sometimes managed to leverage the strategic opportunities opened up by this paradigm (for instance, by working to extend citizenship rights to previously excluded groups). Nevertheless, the political paradigm itself remains at odds with radical conceptions, which must begin (as Marx did) by acknowledging the need to grapple with "men, not in any fantastic isolation or rigidity, but in their actual, empirically perceptible process of development under definite conditions."[15] By drawing on this Marxist insight while simultaneously working to collapse the interval between ontology and politics (by grounding politics in the perceptible processes of perceptible people), autonomous movements discovered a means of cutting to the heart of the bourgeois world.

IV

Suggesting as it does a perfect correspondence between being and doing, this proposition can't help but be seductive. But what, concretely, does it mean in practice? From the standpoint of *Subversion*, securing autonomy meant establishing "the independence of social movements from political parties and trade unions." More fundamental (and thus more abstract) than this organizational premise, however, was the movement's commitment to a "politics of the first person." For Katsiaficas, it is to this commitment that the movement owed its character. Among other things, the politics of the first person were conceived as being antithetical to those "traditional notions" that, in previous times, had prompted revolutionaries to imagine that they could deliver consciousness to the masses.[16] In contrast, autonomists emphasized the need for people to act "according to their own will" using forms of "self-managed consensus" to ensure that actions proceeded "independently of central leaders." According to Katsiaficas, such procedures were "vitally important" to both the movement's self-understanding and to the course it described along its developmental arc.[17]

Concerning that arc, Katsiaficas acknowledges that, along with the politics of the first person, the "material conditions of late capitalism" helped autonomous movements to flourish. Confronted with the redistribution of production throughout the social factory, autonomists began to view centralized parties as being superfluous and "even harmful." In response, they began organizing in ways that reflected "the changed character of society" even as they challenged "the new constellation of power" upon which it was founded.[18] For this reason (and at their threshold), autonomous movements begin for Katsiaficas to suggest the emergence of a new "species universality."[19] At this point, autonomy and the politics of the first person seem paradoxically to presage the absolute.[20]

> In the contemporary world, is there a need for a Leninist centralized organization to bring scientific consciousness to the masses? Or does the conscious spontaneity of the Autonomen contain its own transcendental universality? The organized spontaneity of the squatters' council and other organically generated groups seems to prove that rigidly centralized organizational models are superfluous and even destructive. By creating a form of direct democratic decision-making that necessitates popular involvement, autonomous movements unleash a process that, when allowed to proceed according to its own logic, continually enlarges its constituency and further radicalizes its adherents.[21]

The problem, of course, is that no political operation is ever allowed to proceed solely "according to its own logic." In the end, the Autonomen encountered difficulties when trying to enlarge their constituency, and these difficulties owed in significant part to the logic of struggle to which they adhered. In contrast, when autonomy was most successful, its adherents seemed least beholden to the movement's principled conceptual orientation. Considering the matter retrospectively, it becomes clear that some approaches to struggle are more effective than others despite the fact that each approach may seem (superficially, at least) to embrace the same conceptual premise. Every movement is strung like a bow between its vision and its condition, and only time will tell whether the calibration was right—and whether the movement would hit its mark.

V

As enticing as the promise of a new species universality might seem, the record of *Subversion* remains mixed. Almost from their inception, the struggles recounted by Katsiaficas became imperiled by state repression and fratricidal rancor. For even as the "confrontational politics" favored by the movement "invigorated Germany's political debates" and pushed "single-issue initiatives" toward a more comprehensive struggle,[22] (and even as "the initiative of the Autonomen resulted in larger actions" and created a "context in which other forms of participation...had meaning"[23]), it was also true that autonomy yielded fragmentation all down the line. In one telling moment, Katsiaficas acknowledges that, as movement actions became more militant, "radicals became increasingly autonomous—some would say isolated—from mainstream protests."[24]

Autonomy and isolation: for the movement's heirs, it's easy to gravitate toward those points where practice and principle seen to coincide. What's hard is figuring out how, *as autonomists,* we might participate in "mainstream protests" without reducing them to a mere counterpoint against which to define ourselves. As with Jean-Paul Sartre, who observed that the rebel and the revolutionary could be distinguished by the fact that the former harbored a secret desire to preserve the world so as to define himself against it while the latter transformed that world even at the risk of his own being,[25] autonomy's legacy forces us to consider whether broader movements might be more than a "source of collective identity" rendered in photonegative.[26]

Although it is never stated directly, the question pervading Katsiaficas' work is whether subversion is better served by standing apart on principle or standing together on a terrain riven with contradiction in the name of some greater future synthesis. Describing the decline of Amsterdam's militant squat scene, Katsiaficas recalls how "what had been a feeling of empowerment in 1980" degenerated into "marginalization and paranoia" by the decade's end. This was because, while "conflicts with the system had once been paramount" to movement activity, eventually "the most pressing problems became internal ones." In the end, the movement even became "cut...off from its own membership." As one source reported, the inward turn eventually reduced a vibrant scene with ranks numbering in the thousands to just 200 militants. Then, with "the rest of society...insulated from the movement," numbers dropped further still.[27]

Katsiaficas acknowledges that the tactics and postures that led to this decline tended to "feel good" to those who partook in them. Nevertheless, "they did little to help [the movement] broaden their base of support." Indeed, "the more the Autonomen relied on militant small-group actions, the less popular…they got."[28] Perhaps things would have turned out differently had the movement entered into alliance with other formations; however, since such alliances seemed to violate the logic of autonomy and contradict the politics of the first person, their refusal seems paradoxically to have been both the more principled *and* the easier path to take. In such moments, collapsing the interval between ontology and politics could only mean retreating from the political field and turning inward. At its threshold, this maneuver can't help but presage disappearance.

VI

To get a sense of this dynamic, it suffices to recall the "fight for the Ryesgade," which took place in Copenhagen during the fall of 1986 and serves as the set piece to Katsiaficas' *Subversion* story. Led by the BZ (Occupation Brigade), the battle amounted to what Katsiaficas took to be "the most well-organized single action of the international Autonomen." The fight involved the seizure of an entire neighborhood. Capitalist infrastructure was destroyed and the offices of a company involved in the production of cruise missiles were burnt to the ground. Barricaded defenders repelled successive waves of riot cops with molotov cocktails, bricks, and fireworks.

Inevitably, their actions inspired others, and townsfolk marched on the site to surround the cops after they breached the barricades on one side of the liberated zone. But despite growing neighborhood support and the intensified police violence they confronted, BZ members "easily reached a consensus that reformist solutions…were out of the question." Refusing to "recognize the legitimacy of the government," they "resolved to prove that they were beyond its powers." When the army moved in after nine days of pitched battle to call the BZ's bluff, however, the squatters were forced to modify their approach. At this point, they "called a press conference." But "when the media arrived, they found the houses deserted."[29] A disappearing trick, then, and a fine one at that. Still, one might wonder what message this sent to the townsfolk who had mobilized on the movement's behalf. What power might have been forged (what broader bases of support might have been cultivated) had abstract principle not ruled the day?

I will be the first to admit that stories of the Ryesgade are inspiring. At the same time, they are marked by a kind of bravado—a surfeit of principle—that stands in sharp contrast to the activity that defined the autonomous movement during its ascendance.

VII

Beginning in 1969 and lasting for more than a decade, the German women's movement developed through its struggles against Germany's anti-abortion laws and went on to become central to the political genesis of autonomy.[30] Movement actions included both mass demonstrations against government statutes and the formation of grassroots women's centers. Autonomous in temperament and disposition, the women's movement nevertheless engaged with the state in pursuit of its demands. In a similar fashion, Katsiaficas reports that the autonomous antinuclear campaigns that developed around the same time secured their "first victories...in the courts."[31] These early victories arose from actions that were simultaneously addressed to and directed against the state. And while these struggles fostered an autonomous ethos, the actions in which the movement partook were not yet subordinate to a dogmatism that presupposed that acting *as if* the interval between ontology and politics had been abolished was sufficient for making it so.

Even in the women's movement, however, the ambivalence of autonomy's first premise gradually revealed itself. Consider, for instance, the course traced by the important observation that "the personal is political." A vital insight derived from the feminist struggles of the New Left era, the slogan would go on to become a template for the "politics of the first person" championed by the autonomists. Initially suggesting that our experience of the everyday world could serve as an *analytic* resource (suggesting, for instance, that the social totality could be grasped through its localized and synecdochal manifestation), the slogan envisioned "the personal" more as a transfer medium than as a restricted scale or field of operations. By analyzing the traces that broader social relations left upon this medium, the political character of the total situation could be brought into view. Movement developments indebted to this insight include consciousness-raising groups and auto-nomist theories of the social factory.

But while "the personal is political" started as a radical analytic premise grounded in the materialist tradition, the slo-gan's inflection began to shift over time. In conjunction with its transposition into the "politics of the first person," and as a res-ult of the ambivalence underlying the autonomous movement's first premise (which called on people to collapse the interval between ontology and politics but remained indifferent to the means by which that aim was to be achieved), "the personal" went from being a dynamic field in which "the political" found tangible expression to being the preferred scale for political ac-tion itself. Thus, it was that, despite the movement's initial suc-cesses confronting state power (and despite all that remained to be done), Katsiaficas reports that many participants turned in-ward "to their private spheres of lovers and close friends." And as the meaning of "the personal is political" got "turned on its head," it was almost inevitable that "the new interest in sado-masochism" would gradually take up "more space than [cover-age of] the missile crisis" in movement publications.[32]

VIII

I don't mean to suggest that personal acts are unimportant. As Mohamed Bouazizi's life and death make clear, it's some-times the solitary decision that sets everything in mo-tion—though often in ways we can't predict.[33] But rather than encouraging personal action to be conceived in programmatic or instrumental terms, the movement's "politics of the first per-son" encouraged such acts to be viewed as ends in themselves. As Sartre made clear, self-valorization of this kind is antithetic-al to the revolutionary vocation; nevertheless, it remains con-sistent with autonomy's bid to collapse the interval between ontology and politics. Indeed, since the movement refused to clarify how this aim was to be achieved, and since it refused to establish a line, it provided cover for regressive tendencies to flourish. And so, while both interpretations of "the personal is political" recounted above remain germane when considered from the standpoint of autonomy's first premise, they could not be more different with respect to their practical consequences.

Because they seem to abide by the same spirit, it's easy to imagine that the lesser strategy must share in the greater one's significance. Nevertheless, Katsiaficas' *Subversion* story suggests that not even the movement's ecumenism could conceal the tensions between these orientations or keep participants from grappling with their relative political merits indefinitely. Indeed, "the variety of views within the movement" ensured that its activities were characterized by "lively debate and continual discussion." However, because adherents were "more often oriented to action than to ideology," they felt little need to "fixate on developing a correct line."[34] In the short term, this tendency contributed to the movement's dynamism. However, it also left participants ill-equipped to address the contradictions underlying their first premise. Left unresolved, these contradictions ultimately fostered inertia.

Katsiaficas' interest in foregrounding autonomy's promise and possibility helps to explain why he chose to downplay organization, leadership, and program and align himself with the heterodox eschewal of "correct lines" in *Subversion*. However, it's important to recall that organization played a central role in *The Imagination of the New Left*. In that book, Katsiaficas recounts how, by drawing on the Russian Revolution's organizational form, the Viet Cong set off a global cycle of struggle with the Tet Offensive.[35] For good reason, Katsiaficas underscores the importance of this struggle, which presaged the expulsion of an imperialist aggressor by armed peasant forces. Still, it begs the question: if there is an erotic continuity (as Katsiaficas proposes) between the 1968 cycle and the one recounted in *Subversion*, and if the instigators of '68 were able to play their role in part because of the Leninist inheritance, then what becomes of the organizational forms that could have been transmitted to the autonomists but weren't? How might they have contributed to the movement's development and persistence?

Admitting outright the dangers of authoritarianism and bureaucracy, the historical record nevertheless suggests that revolutionary organization has enabled movements to clarify matters of program and strategy by creating and maintaining frameworks for concrete deliberation. In turn, such deliberation has enabled conscious and decisive action on the political field. As Georg Lukács explains, "on the level of pure theory," the most disparate views and tendencies are able to co-exist peacefully, antagonisms are only expressed in the form of discussions which can be contained within the framework of one and the same organization without disrupting it. But no sooner are these same questions given organizational form than they turn out to be sharply opposed and even incompatible.[36]

Because the autonomous movement eschewed organization and ideological coherence, it was unable (indeed, felt no great need) to resolve the contradictions underlying its foundational concepts and operational premises. Over time, this state of non-resolution pushed the movement toward the less-demanding pole of its founding antinomy, and it was this dynamic that ensured autonomy's decline. And so, while external factors like repression undoubtedly thwarted the movement's advance, we must nevertheless conclude that, logically speaking, its conceptual problems were autonomous too. Arising from the movement's inclinations and shaped by the course it traced across the field of struggle, these problems have become our inheritance—and we must deal with them as such.

IX

Given the alienating character of the bourgeois representational paradigm, autonomy's desire to collapse the interval between ontology and politics is nothing if not sincere. Problems arise, however, when one considers how this aim might best be achieved. The history of *Subversion* reveals that two contradictory tendencies coexisted in autonomous actions. Of these tendencies, the first pointed outward toward confrontation. To be sure, campaigns pursued in this fashion sometimes degenerated into fits of self-valorization; however, they also encouraged decision and concrete reckoning. Consequently, the movement was able in these moments to break with principle so that it could focus more resolutely on questions of analysis and strategy. Autonomy was at its best when it followed this course. The other tendency, which pointed inward, derailed the movement by doubling down on principle and transforming self-valorization into a search for purity. Perhaps it is true, as Katsiaficas has proposed, that both postures are required, and that movements must become points of synthesis where we can "cultivate our capacities to love and to act in an efficient manner—to combine love with mathematical logic."[37] But if this is so, then the tensions between the two outlooks must be laid bare, their content and implications not left to chance. Following Lukács, we might even say that the postures themselves must be given a concrete, organizational form. And if, in the end, "they turn out to be sharply opposed and even incompatible," it would be better to know than to not know.

This is so not least because many of the habits that find expression in contemporary radical movements are clear outgrowths of the postures assumed by autonomy throughout the 1980s. Perversely affirmed by our marginality, our cohort has often gravitated toward modes of autonomous self-valorization that sidestep the demands of the struggles in which we're engaged. Only too late to we discover that, try as we might, the division between ontology and politics will never be resolved through evasion. Stepping out of the political arena to carve out zones of autonomy can help stimulate the imagination and remind us of all that might yet be possible; however, such evasions cannot be how the struggle itself is conducted. Moreover, and at its threshold, disengagement becomes indistinguishable from regression.

In *Subversion*, Katsiaficas reminds us that it was "not uncommon for autonomous groups to borrow images from the world of children." This was because, "in some sense, autonomous groups refuse to grow up: they refuse to shed their dreams of a better world or to conform to existing cultural norms... Their affinity for the pleasure principle—or at least their negation of the reality principle—is a salient part of their identity."[38] A seductive proposition to be sure, but can the limits to which we're alerted by the reality principle really be overcome in this manner? No. The reality from which the reality principle derives can be transformed through practical activity; it cannot, however, be conceptually negated or dodged by retreating into fantasy.[39]

Despite being motivated by a strong desire to collapse the interval between ontology and politics, an evaluation of the movement's developmental arc reveals that its means were inconsistent and even contradictory. And while some approaches proved to be more consequential than others, autonomy's conceptual indeterminacy made it difficult for the matter to be clarified through deliberation and for tactical orientations to be revised. Over time, these factors seem to have encouraged participants to avoid confrontations that were not ends in themselves so that they might double down on a narrow, self-valorizing conception of the politics of the first person. The result was a political orientation that, despite invoking autonomy's pedigree, proved incompatible with the vibrant confrontations and outward orientation that had enabled the movement to win its most tangible victories.

When approached symptomatically, the lessons of *Subversion* suggest that collapsing the interval between ontology and politics can only be achieved by attacking the bourgeois representational paradigm directly. Here, challenges to constituted power must include efforts to cultivate relationships with those who still fall within its purview. Both the principled demonstration of freedom in action and the awareness that we won't make it alone are required. And strategy, for its part, must be developed not on the basis of principle but of analysis. In short, the movement's "first person" must not be singular but plural, not "I" but "we." This first person is not a "being" to be valorized but a "becoming" to be produced.

X

There's much that contemporary radicals can learn from autonomy. And given the challenges we confront, we must find inspiration where we can. Reviewing Katsiaficas' *Subversion* story, however, makes clear that the movement may well be at its most valuable when approached from the standpoint of its failures. For all its disruptive force, the autonomous movement was unable to clarify the meaning and implications of its first premise. It allowed for contradictory tendencies to emerge and even for the lesser of those tendencies to prevail. Movements today are similarly suspicious of organization and correct lines; how will we ensure that our temperament does not lead us to reprise past failures?

Will our politics lead to a valorized being or a productive becoming? And will the "first person" around whom we organize be singular or plural? Of these two options, the latter is admittedly more demanding, but it is also the one that holds revolution in its heart. The autonomous movement's inward turn and its confusion regarding the meaning of the "politics of the first person" allowed for an asocial, purely Romantic conception of revolution to flourish. And while this line may have contributed to the valorization of its initiates, it became an impediment to the development of the movement's revolutionary force. Considering the political field on which we now operate, it's evident that many of these problems have persisted. Making sense of autonomy's failures can help us to navigate the challenges we now confront, but only if we can acknowledge that their desires became ensnared by principles that would never do them justice.

Endnotes

1 George Katsiaficas, *The Imagination of the New Left: A Global Analysis of 1968* (Cambridge, MA: South End Press, 1987).

2 George Katsiaficas, *The Subversion of Politics: European Autonomous Movements and the Decolonization of Everyday Life* (Oakland: AK Press, 2006), 8.

3 *Upping the Anti: A Journal of Theory and Action*, n.d., n.p., http://uppingtheanti.org.

4 AK Thompson, "Remembering May '68: An Interview with George Katsiaficas," *Upping the Anti: A Journal of Theory and Action*, Number Six, 2008.

5 AK Thompson, *Black Bloc, White Riot: Anti-Globalization and the Genealogy of Dissent* (Oakland: AK Press, 2010).

6 Jason Del Gandio and AK Thompson (eds.), *Spontaneous Combustion: The Eros Effect and Global Revolution* (Albany: SUNY Press, 2017).

7 According to Katsiaficas, while the analysis of the circulation of struggle "can help us to trace how one thing causes another, which causes another in turn," it fails to capture the manner in which struggles "produce feedback loops with multiple iterations." Whereas "the circulation of struggles describes the process of movement development geometrically," the eros effect "describes these same developments in terms of calculus." AK Thompson, "Remembering May '68: An Interview with George Katsiaficas," *Upping the Anti: A Journal of Theory and Action*," Number 6, May 2008, 62–63.

8 George Katsiaficas, *The Subversion of Politics*, 217–233.

9 Ibid.

10 Ibid., 128.

11 George Katsiaficas, *The Subversion of Politics*, x.

12 Ibid., 128.

13 Ibid., 74

14 Ibid., 195.

15 Karl Marx and Friedrich Engels, *The German Ideology* (New York: International Publishers, 1976), 47.

16 George Katsiaficas, *The Subversion of Politics*, 7.

17 Ibid., 8.

18 Ibid., 15.

19 Ibid.

20 There is a strand of liberal political philosophy that maintains that the rational pursuit of self-interest can lead to social harmony; however, this position tends to be refuted by radicals, who prefer to emphasize the conflicts of interest that prevail within stratified societies. Marx once encouraged his readers to consider the "indefinite prodigiousness of their own aims," but this conception presupposed a move through conflict toward absolution. By linking the politics of the first person to "a new species universality," Katsiaficas professes his allegiance to this approach; however, nothing requires that the politics of the first person be conceptualized in this way. In the worst iterations, the concept can even encourage historical stasis by legitimating self preservation. The problem becomes clear when one recalls how, for Adorno, "self-preservation annuls all life." Karl Marx, "The Eighteenth Brumaire of Louis Bonaparte," *Selected Works, Volume 1* (Moscow: Progress Publishers, 1969), 401; Theodor Adorno, *Minima Memoria: Reflections on a Damaged Life* (New York: Verso, 2005), 229.

21 George Katsiaficas, *The Subversion of Politics*, 102.

22 Ibid., 195.

23 Ibid., 128.

24 Ibid., 87.

25 Jean-Paul Sartre, *Baudelaire* (New York: New Directions Publishing, 1950), 51–52.

26 George Katsiaficas, *The Subversion of Politics*, 87.

27 Ibid., 117.

28 Ibid., 124.

29 Ibid., 123.

30 Ibid., 69–72.

31 Ibid., 83.

32 George Katsiaficas, *The Subversion of Politics*, 78–79.

33 To learn more about Bouazizi and the effect his act of self immolation had on world history, see Rebecca Solnit, "Letter to a Dead Man About the Occupation of Hope," Tom Dispatch, October 18, 2011, https://tomdispatch.com/rebecca-solnit-this-land-is-your-occupied-land/

34 Ibid., 192.

35 George Katsiaficas, *The Imagination of the New Left*, 19.

36 Georg Lukács, *History and Class Consciousness* (Cambridge, MA: The MIT Press, 1971), 299.

37 AK Thompson, "Remembering May '68," 66.

38 Ibid., 132.

39 Psychoanalysts have often treated neuroses by prompting patients to become aware of their desire while acknowledging the practical reasons that their resolution may be socially untenable. Here, repression isn't dissolved so much as managed through the process of conscious election. At best, the thwarted desire is guided toward forms of sublimation. But while this therapeutic orientation suggests a strong conservative current in psychoanalysis, it is by no means the tradition's only tendency. Indeed, as Freud argued in his essay "On the Question of Lay Analysis," "the ego learns that there is yet another way of securing satisfaction besides adaptation to the external world which I have described. It is also possible to intervene in the world by changing it and to establish in it intentionally the conditions which make satisfaction possible. This activity then becomes the ego's highest function; decisions as to when it is more expedient to control one's passions and bow before reality, and when it is more expedient to side with them and to take arms against the external world—such decisions make up the whole essence of worldly wisdom" (New York: W.W. Norton & Company, 1978), 24.

References

Adorno, T. (2005). *Minima Memoria: Reflections on a Damaged Life*, New York: Verso.

Del Gandio, J., and AK Thompson (eds.) (2017). *Spontaneous Combustion: The Eros Effect and Global Revolution*, Albany: SUNY Press.

Freud, S., (1978). *On the Question of Lay Analysis*, New York: W.W. Norton & Company.

Katsiaficas, G. (1987). *The Imagination of the New Left: A Global Analysis of 1968*, Cambridge, MA: South End Press.

Katsiaficas, G. (2006). *The Subversion of Politics: European Autonomous Movements and the Decolonization of Everyday Life*, Oakland: AK Press.

Lukács, G. (1971). *History and Class Consciousness*, Cambridge, MA: The MIT Press.

Marx, K. (1969). "The Eighteenth Brumaire of Louis Bonaparte," *Selected Works, Volume 1*, Moscow: Progress Publishers.

Marx, K., and F. Engels (1976). *The German Ideology*, New York: International Publishers.

Sartre, J.-P. (1950). *Baudelaire*, New York: New Directions Publishing.

Solnit, R. (2011). "Letter to a Dead Man About the Occupation of Hope," *Tom Dispatch*, October 18, 2011, https://tomdispatch.com/rebecca-solnit-this-land-is-your-occupied-land/

Thompson, AK. (2008). "Remembering May '68: An Interview with George Katsiaficas," *Upping the Anti: A Journal of Theory and Action*, Number Six.

Thompson, AK. (2010). *Black Bloc, White Riot: Anti-Globalization and the Genealogy of Dissent*, Oakland: AK Press.

Chapter 3

The Autonomy of Struggles and the Self-Management of Squats:
Legacies of Intertwined Movements[*]

Miguel A. Martínez
Uppsala University, Sweden

Once squatters' movements become visible, articulated, durable and challenging to the status quo, there is an increasing elaboration of political discourse. This process is usually controversial, both internally and externally. Not all branches or factions of the movements agree with the major narratives about the nature of squatting. Some of these narratives in circulation are so intimately related to academic debates that the boundaries between both realms can also appear relatively blurred. This is the case with the notions of "'autonomy" and an "autonomous movement" which have permeated many theoretical understandings of squatting over time, despite the indifference or disdain of some activists. In this chapter I argue that autonomist approaches have widely circulated among squatters all over Europe and provided an often implicit or vague identity for most of them. However, what is the meaning of autonomy? By revisiting the accounts of autonomist and squatters' movements in Italy, Germany and Spain, I will show the relevance of the social aspects of autonomy, which are sometimes obscured by more individualistic interpretations. In addition, I suggest that anti-capitalist stances, feminism, and solidarity with migrants have significantly contributed to the ideological meaning of autonomy, which has especially influenced the way squatters—especially their most politicized branches—manage their

* *Originally published in* Interface: A Journal for and About Social Movements, *Vol. 11 (1): 178 – 199 (July 2019). We thank the author and* Interface *for authorizing us to reprint this paper.*

occupied spaces. This approach delineates the prevailing left-libertarian tenets as well as the squatting practices of houses and social centers, while helping to distinguish them from the extraordinary cases of far-right squats.

Autonomist politics emerged first from radical workers' struggles, but squatters followed suit. During the 1960s and 1970s, squatting combined autonomist, countercultural, and feminist inputs, although the latter are not so frequently highlighted by the literature. The connection of struggles across urban territory and different social issues found fertile ground in the squatted social centers, usually in tight connection with housing campaigns and squatting actions too. Principles, memories, and examples from these autonomous experiences were adopted by the global justice movement around 2000 and, again, by the anti-austerity mobilizations a decade later (Flesher 2014), which indicates their long-lasting influence.

In my interpretation, the main misunderstanding about autonomism is the role played by "individual autonomy" as a "politics of the first person," a "politics of desire" or the prevalence of individuals over organizations (Flesher 2007, Gil 2011, Katsiaficas 2006, Pruijt and Roggeband 2014). Although most authors mention this individualistic feature to distinguish autonomism from the more authoritarian, hierarchical, and bureaucratic organizations of the institutional left, I do not find this view very informative. Instead, as I shall argue, the expression "social autonomy" seems to capture more accurately the central concerns of the collective practice of horizontal direct democracy and self-management fostered by autonomists. Even the feminist insights reveal that issues usually considered personal and private are politicized by making them socially visible and publicly debated. In addition, the radical independence of both the struggles and the oppressed groups is always voiced in a relational manner, not as individual independence: first, by identifying the social sources and dynamics of oppression; and second, and in a collective way, by empowering those who cooperate with each other in order to get rid of their perceived oppressions. More than a tension between the individual and the social dimensions present in all social phenomena, I argue that it is the specific emphasis given to the political method of autonomism (self-organization and self-management, autonomy from capitalism, patriarchy and racism) and their immediatist engagement in various contentious campaigns that makes it distinct compared to other political identities.

Although massive occupations of houses took place in some European countries in the aftermath of the Second World War, and many housing movements resorted to squatting as their main protest action (Aguilera 2018, Bailey 1973, Mudu 2014), squatters' movements developed their autonomist bases starting in the mid-1960s with the eruption of countercultural groups such as the Provos in the Netherlands (Dadusc 2017: 24, Smart 2014: 113) and the Situationist International group (see, for example, Debord 1967, Knabb 1997, Sadler 1998). Moreover, feminism provided a framework to challenge everyday life around social reproduction and housework beyond the housing question at large (with regards to provision, access, affordability, policies, etc.). However, the self-management of social relations and spaces within squatted houses and social centers did not imply a fully liberated space from capitalism, patriarchy, and racism (Kadir 2016). Feminist groups and campaigns thus proved crucial in persuading autonomists and squatters of the need to incorporate their demands into radical politics (Bhattacharya et al. 2017, Federici 2012, Fraser 2008).

In the next sections, I review the main references in the literature that help to make my case. Only three countries are selected (two from Southern Europe and one from the North), but it suffices to disentangle the intertwined relations of autonomist struggles and the historical origins of the notion of autonomy. I recall this debate because I noticed its legacies in the squats I visited, read about, or joined as an activist during the past two decades all over Europe. However, the allusions to the autonomist notions and related events were seldom unequivocal.

Italy: From the Factory to Metropolitan Struggles

The influences of anarchism, heterodox (anti-state) Marxism, anti-institutionalism, and countercultural anti-authoritarian politics in the "new social movements" and the "new left" after 1968 were pervasive in squatting activism, although at different paces in each country (Van der Steen et al. 2014). These first trends of a vague autonomist movement had another precedent in the Italian Marxist-inspired *Operaismo* (workerism).

This intellectual and political group had been sowing the seeds of autonomist politics since the early 1960s by focusing on the autonomy of workers' struggles from political parties and from labor unions. They also launched activist self-research (called *coricerca*) with factory workers and favored wildcat strikes, absenteeism, and sabotage on the assembly line (Balestrini and Moroni 1997, Katsiaficas 2006: 17–57). Leftist intellectuals and students engaged with class struggles in which the lowest tiers of the proletariat and the workers' viewpoint were expected to take the lead. A full opposition to salaried work and an invitation to take over the factories were a decisive inspiration for those who started occupying empty buildings and setting up squatted self-managed social centres (*Centri Sociali*) some years later, especially around the large mobilization peaks of 1967–69 and 1976–77.

This move, as Geronimo recalls, had its roots in the defeat of many labor struggles, the transformation of the productive system and the rise of the precarious class, which merged impoverished university graduates, casual workers, and unemployed people. As Geronimo explains, militants "looted supermarkets... rode public transport for free, refused to pay for rock concerts and movie screenings... [and some] used guns... ravaged hotels, and hundreds of cars and buses [were] toppled and torched" (Geronimo 2012: 42–45). Both Geronimo and Kastiaficas (2006: 65–66, 188) acknowledge that the Italian *Autonomia* was so influential in German extra-parliamentary politics that these activists changed their own name to the *Autonomen* by 1979–80. Danish political squatters did the same in the late-1980s, precisely when most political squats were evicted and anti-fascism, anti-racism, and anti-imperialism replaced the priority hitherto enjoyed by squatting (Karpantschof and Mikkelsen 2014: 188–193).

Workerism was the origin of autonomism, but the occupations of houses and social centers, along with tenants' struggles, were already in place and often supported by the Italian Communist Party (Mudu and Rossini 2018: 100). The turn to autonomism started with a wave of occupations around 1968, especially in large cities such as Milan. For example, located in Piazza Fontana, the very heart of the city, was the squatted "Ex Hotel Commercio." Run by university students in alliance with many political groups and the local tenants' union, it was considered "the largest urban commune... in Europe" (Balestrini and Moroni 1997: 276; Martin and Moroni 2007). Despite the call for the autonomy of the struggles, and as a reaction to harsh state repression and several fascist murders (Balestrini and Moroni 1997: 363, 542), workerist activists set up multiple extra-parliamentary parties and organizations (Lotta Continua, Potere Operaio, Avanguardia Operaia, etc.) over the 1970s who joined anarchists, feminists, situationists, students, and housing activists in the squatted social centres of the following decades. These groups were short-lived, but their promotion of workers' autonomy has left a strong legacy among squatters, mainly since 1973. As Balestrini and Maroni maintain, "the proletarian sociality defines its own laws and practices in the territory that the bourgeoisie occupies by force" (Balestrini and Moroni 1997: 451).

Consequently, beyond independence from electoral and institutional politics, autonomists fostered the autonomy of workers' power, knowledge, cooperation, needs, resistance, and struggles in order to take back the time, money, and spaces from the hands of the capitalist class. A diffuse political identity, multiple points of conflicts and insurrections, and decentralized actions aimed at mobilizing large amounts of the proletariat were translated into the politicization of new squatting waves from the mid-1980s onwards (Mudu and Rossini 2018: 101).

The Indiani Metropolitani and the Circoli del Proletariato Giovanile represented one of the countercultural echelons that connected autonomist politics and squatting. For example, a celebrated pamphlet of the latter from 1977 declared, "We want it all! It's time to rebel!... We occupy buildings because we want to have meeting places to debate, to play music and do theatre, to have a specific and alternative place for family life" (Balestrini and Moroni 1997: 524). In addition to demands for affordable housing, the constraints experienced through conservative family traditions, a deep opposition to commodified and state-controlled leisure as well as the alienation engendered by salaried work motivated this mixture of autonomism and, often joyful and satiric, Situationism applied to urban squatting.

Internal ideological controversies among squatters adhered to different branches of autonomism, anarchism, and feminism were very frequent, but they also contributed to the creation of a vibrant political milieu in many cities (Mudu 2009: 217–225, 2012: 416–418). In contrast to Anglo-Saxon countries—where anarchism and autonomism are almost synonyms—both branches had different historical trajectories and stances in Italy and Spain (Mudu 2012: 414–418). During the 1977 protest waves, for example, both shared an anti-authoritarian approach, but autonomists tended to lead and hegemonize the movement (Mudu 2012: 417).

Nonetheless, in my interpretation, the collective self-management of squats, either for living or for socialization, and in tight connection with the autonomy of the working-class and oppressed groups, represents the best theoretical and political coincidence among all the overtly politicized squatters. This has hardly been noted in the literature on autonomous politics where squats are often seen as just another strand of activism (Wennerhag et al. 2018). However, due to the decline of struggles at the workplace, the self-management of squats all over the metropolitan area took the lead, affecting different spheres of social life and helping to unite anarchists, punks, and autonomists in the second-generation social centers during the mid-1980s, as argued too by Mudu (2012: 420) and Piazza (2018: 503).

In short, by considering all the above insights, a dominant politics of what I designate as "social autonomy" increasingly found its own way, its own proponents, and its own practitioners in urban politics beyond the institutional labor unions and the parliamentary political parties of the left. Furthermore, this notion was also crucially nurtured by feminism.

Although less mentioned by the literature, during the 1960s and 1970s an innovative and challenging feminist movement emerged in tight connection with Italian autonomism. Active women in leftist politics called for their self-organization without men involved in their groups, meetings, or protest actions. By doing so, they were able to politicize many issues conventionally considered personal and private, such as housework, sexuality, and violence against women. These topics were not yet at the center of institutional feminism, which at the time was more focused on gender equality in terms of voting rights, access to education, and managerial positions. As Federici explains:

> We learned to seek the protagonists of class struggle not only among the male industrial proletariat but, most importantly, among the enslaved, the colonized, the world of wageless workers marginalized by the annals of the communist tradition to whom we could now add the figure of the proletarian housewife, reconceptualized as the subject of the (re)production of the workforce. (Federici 2012: 7)

Autonomous feminists contributed to identifying housework as a pillar of the social-metropolitan factory. Instead of a consideration of domestic life as informal social relations or mere consumption, reproductive labor, even under a wageless condition, was seen as crucial for the continuation of capitalism. Adding to the state provision of welfare services (like education, health, pensions, subsidies, etc.), feminists revealed that the production of meals, shopping, cleaning, having and raising children, taking care of the ill and the elderly, etc. was reproductive work, or housework, and it was an arena where women are oppressed, hidden, and dismissed by other male-driven struggles (Federici 2012: 18–19).

Campaigns such as Wages for Housework during the 1970s, demonstrations for the right to abortion and marches to "re-appropriate the night" (Balestrini and Moroni 1997: 499) initiated a long-lasting wave of autonomous feminism that pervaded most squats as well as autonomist and anarchist groups. The frustrating experience of the sexual division of labor within radical organizations and the dominance of men when it comes to speaking out and writing, in addition to other forms of sexism in leftist politics, motivated the creation of female-only groups, campaigns, demonstrations, and squats (Balestrini and Moroni 1997: 491–494, 506; Martin and Moroni 2007: 162–163). Autonomy meant a separation from men that was conceived as a necessary step to demystify femininity, to make visible women's subjugation and resistance, and to further forge the unity of all the social categories of subordinated groups, including workers, but also gay people, sex workers, ethnic minorities, migrants, etc. Autonomy also implied an exercise of women's power apart from state institutions, even from dominant discourses about women's rights. As Federici explains, "feminism risks becoming an institution" (Federici 2012: 61).

To appreciate the shifting contents of autonomy, it is also worth mentioning that Italian post-autonomist groups split during the 1990s into various factions (with anarchists also taking sides) mainly due to three contested issues that constrained the reach of self-management: the legalization of squats, the participation of radical activists in electoral politics, and the introduction of waged employees in social centers. Individual autonomy was a key basis for many anarchists who, in turn, were less interested in the social dimension of class struggles. Individual leadership was criticized by all, but it was not a significant issue for many post-autonomist groups represented by well-known spokespersons. The call to "exit the ghetto" of the squats and reach out to a larger social sphere indicated a crucial concern for all kinds of radical activists—the size and scale of the social feature of autonomous struggles.

Therefore, the Italian radical-left scene was subject to "both movements of convergence and divergence between post-autonomists and anarchists" (Mudu 2012: 421). A landmark moment that signaled the main division between anarchist and post-autonomist squatters was the 2001 anti-G8 mobilization in Genoa. Since then, their mutual interactions in practice have been scarce and limited to broader campaigns, such as the NO-TAV struggle against the high-speed train to connect Italy and France (Della Porta and Piazza 2008) and the referendum against the privatization of water (Mudu 2012: 422). However, recent developments of squatted social centers and houses over the 2010s have kept reproducing the tenets of social autonomy while adding new meanings and tensions. For example, housing movements have included more subaltern groups such as poor migrants and homeless people in the squatting movement (Aureli and Mudu 2018, Feliciantonio 2017, Grazioli and Caciagli 2018).

The occupations of abandoned theaters and cinemas stirred larger political debates on the grassroots production of culture as a common good and the increasing precarious working conditions of the youth (Maddanu 2018, Valli 2015, Piazza 2018). Although these experiences remained attached to the legacies of autonomous self-organization of oppressed groups and their active involvement in the self-management of squats, they were more prone to negotiating legal agreements with the authorities, and more experienced activists often led the initiatives.

Germany: Mobilization and Liberation of Everyday Life

Even before being adopted as a political identity, autonomism in West Germany reshaped extra-parliamentary politics and urban struggles in a different manner compared to the new social movements that had already emerged around 1968. For example, instead of focusing on self-management, Katsiaficas recalled situationist and Lefebvrian concepts—"alienation" and "everyday life," above all—to define autonomy in that context. "By 1980," he explains:

> ...a movement existed which was clearly more radical and bigger than that of the sixties. The new movement was more diverse and unpredictable, and less theoretical and organized than was the New Left. Despite their differences, they shared a number of characteristics; anti-authoritarianism; independence from existing political parties; decentralized organizational forms; emphasis on direct action. (Katsiaficas (2006: 3–6)

Katsiaficas' interpretation of autonomist ideas in Germany highlights two aspects that might resemble individualistic views of autonomy: the "politics of the first person" and the "decolonization of everyday life." Within the autonomist scenes, individuals would feel free from party discipline, state control, capitalist-induced compulsive consumerism, and patriarchal domination. However, he also insists that German autonomist activists were well organized in small groups of militants and as a coherent movement. Furthermore, his definition also included self-managed consensus, open assemblies without leaders and spontaneous forms of militant resistance to domination in all realms of life, society, and politics, which very much resembles the collectivist anarchism approach (Ward and Goodway 2014). Despite the frequent references to the politics of the first person, autonomy is defined as collective relationships, or social autonomy on my terms, not as individual subjectivity. Katsiaficas explains that "the Autonomen see their ideas as a revolutionary alternative to both authoritarian socialism (Soviet-style societies) and 'pseudodemocratic capitalism'... The Autonomen seek to change governments as well as everyday life, to overthrow capitalism and patriarchy" (Katsiaficas 2006: 8).

But what is "everyday life?" How can it be decolonized? According to Katsiaficas, everyday life is the sphere of civil society which is separate from state institutions. It is also a political sphere where direct democracy is possible in contrast to both the delegation of power to formal organizations and aspirations to conquer state power. Activism focused on everyday life tries to change the whole political and economic system through direct actions against established powers but, at the same time, against its manifestations in every domain of life (education, family life, friendship, dwelling, workplaces, and urban settings in general). Hence, Katsiaficas defines autonomism as an emergent social movement aiming to promote feminism, migrant rights, and worker cooperatives—for example, while suggesting that autonomy opposes universalizing forms of oppression (Katsiaficas 2006: 14–16, 238).

In particular, what he designates as the "colonization of everyday life" refers to the rise of "instrumental rationality" worldwide. This means that the forces of capital intend to commodify every aspect of our lives and needs (such as food, shelter, air, water, communication, mobility, affects, etc.) and make profit out of it.

Individualization, atomization, privatization, and alienation are the tools used by the capitalist colonizers. As a response, collective autonomy as it is represented in squats appeals to the emancipatory will of youth, women, ethnic minorities, and precarious workers. "Communal living," Katsiaficas states, "expands the potential for individual life choices and creates the possibility of new types of intimate relationships and new models of child rearing" (Katsiaficas 2006: 247).

Although there is no agreement about the meaning of autonomism, the theses formulated by German activists in 1981 are eloquent:

> We fight for ourselves and others fight for themselves... We do not engage in "representative struggles." Our activities are based on our affectedness, "politics of the first person"... We fight for a self-determined life in all aspects of our exist-

ence, knowing that we can only be free if all are free. We do not engage in dialogue with those in power!... We all embrace a "vague anarchism" but we are not anarchists in a traditional sense. We have no organization per se... Short-term groups form to carry out an action or to attend protests. Long-term groups form to work on continuous projects. (Geronimo 2012: 174)

This political approach led to solid opposition to fascism, imperialism, and capitalism on the one hand, but also to the creation of lasting networks of self-managed occupied houses, social centers, women's groups, and cooperative initiatives on the other. The influence of Italian autonomism was noted in some publications and debates of various political groups during the 1970s, which sometimes intersected with the squatting initiatives of the decade (Geronimo 2012: 48–57, 61–66).

However, more elaborate contents were explicitly added to the German version of autonomism in the early 1980s due to the resurgence of squatters' mobilizations (Geronimo 2012: 99–106). Originally, the remnants of 1968 anti-authoritarianism and the new peace, environmental, and feminist movements merged with multiple residents' protests (*Bürgerinitiativen*) all over the country and with countercultural situationist-inspired politics, such as the *Spontis*. Katsiaficas explains that:

Like the Metropolitan Indians in Italy, *Spontis* loved to poke fun at their more serious "comrades" and used irony rather than rationality to make their point. In 1978, *Spontis* in Münster helped elect a pig to a university office, and in Ulm, a dog was nominated to the Academic Senate. (Katsiaficas 2006: 63, 65)

In this milieu, according to Katsiaficas, feminists centrally contributed to the definition of autonomy (Katsiaficas 2006: 67). They fought for the decriminalization of abortion, equal pay for equal work, housing affordability, shelters for women subject to intimate partner violence and public subsidies for mothers. They also focused on a radical change in the sphere of everyday life, demanding that men (activists included) share domestic labor with women, creating self-help groups, launching campaigns to "take back the night" and setting up feminist publications, centers, and residential spaces (squatted ones included) in which men were not allowed (Gaillard 2013). Indeed, "from the first big squatting wave in 1980/81, in which more than 200 houses in total were occupied, until 2013, around 20 houses in West Berlin and (united) Berlin have been squatted by female/ lesbian/ gay/ queer/ trans people" (azozomox 2014: 190).

Their large mobilizations, direct actions and even guerrilla groups added new meanings to what I term "social autonomy" as women's power against male violence and complete independence from hierarchical structures and institutions (Katsiaficas 2006: 74–75). Although the motto "the personal is political" might obscure this collective dimension, it was the politicization of all hitherto considered private topics and everyday life, by questioning the social domination inside them and by making it visible, that justifies their autonomist insight.

Two other specific components of the German political context were the long-lasting peace and anti-nuclear movements first, and the institutionalization and co-optation of a substantial share of those activists by the Green Party next. Members of those camps, as well as the Autonomen, were less involved with workers' struggles than their Italian counterparts due to the more generous welfare state and labour unions effective in obtaining concessions, which softened the precarious condition of many activists and attracted more middle-class people to activism as well.

However, squatting became a key icon for the autonomists, and, in neighborhoods such as Kreuzberg in Berlin, poor Turkish immigrants, marginalized youth, punks, gays, and artists also became fully engaged in the movement. Katsiaficas writes:

> They were more a motley collection than a self-defined collectivity of mainly students like the New Left was. As living behind barricades became a way of life for many squatters, the illegality of their everyday lives radicalized their attitude toward the state." (Katsiaficas 2006: 91, 168–173)

From the late 1970s to the early 1980s, squatters took over hundreds of houses—at least in the large cities—performed street fighting and demonstrations in which the black color was dominant in both flags and dress codes, and created leaderless organizations, although they also had to face harsh police attacks, arrests, and prosecution. This phase ended in partial legalizations that depoliticized part of the movement (Holm and Kuhn 2011). The movement still, however, kept squatting as the primary identity sign for its remaining militant wing, especially where it was considered a victory against overwhelming repression, such as the Hafenstrasse squatted buildings in Hamburg in the late 1980s (Katsiaficas 2006: 91–96, 124–128, 178).

More generally, it is also worth recalling that another attempt to define autonomism in 1983 combined the general anti-capitalist stance with concern about all forms of domination:

> Aspiring autonomy means first of all to struggle against political and moral alienation in life and work... This is expressed when houses are squatted to live in dignity and to avoid paying outrageous rent; it is expressed when workers stay at home because they no longer tolerate the control at the workplace; it is expressed when the unemployed loot supermarkets. (Geronimo 2012: 115)

This author engages with the view of autonomy as collective self-determination. This implies the capacity of every social group to define the norms that will rule their own collective life. Most people are deprived from this right and basic source of power in both representative and authoritarian regimes, although to different extents. In so doing, autonomists need to deliberate in public, justify their stances and reach consensus. This intense process of communication occurs prior to making decisions about the norms and actions to follow.

Eventually, autonomists had a contradictory relationship with the post-1968 alternative movement that became one of the moderate electoral bases for the Greens and for social-democratic politics. Although food cooperatives, bars, bookstores, cultural events, self-managed clinics, playgrounds, etc. formed a convenient and ideologically sympathetic environment for autonomists, they usually criticized alternative infrastructures and enterprises because of their limited anti-capitalist impact (Geronimo 2012: 103–105). The contributions of autonomism to squatting were also accompanied with conflicts of violence among activists; sexism, homophobia, and transphobia (azozomox 2014); subtle forms of social control and homogenization within the scene; extreme measures to prevent police infiltration; and even a nihilist rejection of intellectual analyses and affirmative political alternatives (Katsiaficas 2006: 177–180; Geronimo 2012: 174).

Squatting movements in Germany unfolded especially during the early 1980s and, after a combined policy of legalization and repression of new squatting attempts, at the crossroads of its reunification with former East Germany, around 1990 (Holm and Kuhn 2011). As an illustration, between 1979 and 1984, there were 287 squatted houses and wagon places in West Berlin (azozomox and Kuhn 2018: 148). Another peak was reached between 1989 and 1991 when 214 buildings were squatted in Berlin, mostly in the former Eastern boroughs (azozomox and Kuhn 2018: 152). The issue of the squat legalization was highly controversial and engendered splits among autonomists of the first period, but it became more widely accepted after the 1990s. In cities such as Hamburg, the language of social autonomy permeates both legalized initiatives (Hafenstrasse in the late 1980s and Gängeviertel in the 2010s) and those partially tolerated (Rote Flora), but the strains with the authorities' attempts to institutionalize and co-opt autonomist activists keep going. On the one hand, the large numbers of legalized squats in those periods granted the Autonomen a long-lasting material infrastructure for continuing their political projects and struggles. On the other hand, although the German autonomists remained the main proponents and supporters of squatting actions, the more repressive contexts forced them to shift focus towards other campaigns, such as solidarity with migrants, anti-capitalist summits, environmental protests, tenants' rights, anti-fascism, and feminist claims at all the levels of politics.

Spain: Diffused Autonomy and Interdependence

Autonomism was well spread in other European countries such as Spain. The fascist dictatorship that lasted from 1936–9 to 1975 made a striking difference compared to other Western political regimes based on liberal democracy. Many workers' unions and strikes had to operate underground until the late 1970s when they unfolded massively in most industrial areas. Despite the hegemony of the Spanish Communist Party in many of these struggles, workers' autonomous organizations and assemblies were quite significant in many sectors. Extra-parliamentary politics also consisted of manifold leftist organizations that often engaged with the demands of residents in urban neighborhoods (Castells 1983).

The practice of squatting buildings was not very frequent, but the revival of anarchism contributed to the establishment of Ateneos Libertarios, occupied social centers run by anarchist unions and various affinity groups, and countercultural social centers (inspired by the hippy and alternative movements around 1968) in the period known as "transition to democracy" that lasted until the early 1980s (Martínez 2018, Seminario 2014: 23–77).

During the first wave of political squatting in the mid-1980s, the autonomist identity was more imported from round-trip visits to Italy, Germany, and Holland than linked to their own legacy of autonomous factory struggles. Many squatters also preferred to associate their ideological roots with the core vigorous anarchist tradition from the decades before the dictatorship, which sometimes produced frictions with the vague anarchism and heterodox-Marxism embraced by the autonomists. Against this backdrop, it is worth mentioning that the successful anti-militarist movement at that time (Martínez 2007: 380) achieved a high legitimation of non-violent direct action among most social movements, especially those who fully supported the anti-conscription campaign like most autonomists and squatters. In addition, nationalist/independentist militants and members of Left parties took part in some squats or initiated their own, especially in Catalonia, Galicia, and the Basque Country.

An autonomous branch of the feminist movement was also very active over the decades and was especially engaged in the squatters' movement, even founding their own social centers exclusively for women, such as Matxarda, La Karbonera, and Andretxe in the Basque Country (Padrones 2017: 227–235); Eskalera Karakola in Madrid (squatted in 1996, legalized in 2005); and La Morada-La Fresca in Barcelona (1997–8) (Gil 2011: 77–97). In a similar vein to what happened in Italy and Germany, there were endless debates between diffuse and organized forms of autonomy, especially among those who participated in the political scene around *Lucha Autónoma* in Madrid (Casanova 2002, Seminario 2014: 121–182).

By 1987, the autonomists had presented a political agenda with an explicit social orientation in the squatted social center

Arregui y Aruej based on self-management, anti-authoritarianism, direct action, and anti-capitalism (Casanova 2002: 36–37). During the next decade and a half, squatted social centers and houses became a focal point of activity for all the autonomists, but there were many more squats in which autonomy was no more than a package of multiple radical ideas in circulation. Anti-fascism as a political priority, for example, distinguished a certain number of squats from the rest (Seminario 2014: 130–131), which denotes the existence of significant social and political diversity in the squatters' movement. However, the regular practice of assemblies, direct democracy, self-organization and engagement with numerous social struggles around the squats disseminated a diffuse politics of social autonomy among the most active and politicized squatters (Salamanca et al. 2012).

An abundant publication of short pamphlets, fanzines (such as *Resiste, Sabotaje, El Acratador, Ekintza Zuzena, Etcétera, Contrapoder,* etc.), and some radical newspapers occasionally served to discuss theoretical and political aspects of autonomism. In Madrid, the squatted social center Laboratorio (initiated in 1997) was one of the most prolific in recalling the post-workerist views and engaging with the Zapatista uprising (1994 to date) and its anti-neoliberal discourse. Their mandate was:

> ...to experiment with how to embed the squatted social centres in the metropolitan territory: struggles against real estate speculation, against the deterioration of the urban peripheries, against the expulsion of residents in the city center, against the militarization of the land and CCTV surveillance, against total institutions, against the authoritarianism of urban planning, against new forms of fascism... We aim to express the potential of an insubordinate life facing the void of capital...forms of cooperation against hierarchy, control and separation. (Casanova 2002: 162–163)

As in Italy, precarious young workers and students were the most active social composition of the squatters' movement, although residents of all ages, migrants, artists, and activists from many other social movements were often drawn to the squats. Therefore, anti-capitalism and concerns about labor conditions (precariousness) were crucial in their political approach to reclaim urban spaces and neighborhoods.

In addition, the autonomist branch of Spanish feminism since the 1980s was intimately attached to squatting (see, for example, their publication *Mujeres Preokupando*), although not all the groups occupied spaces, and their political concerns were much broader (Gil 2011, Seminario 2014: 303–357).

Interestingly, they nurtured autonomist urban politics by building upon insights from other international trends of radical feminism and by raising debates that were beyond the usual agenda of squatters. On the one hand, autonomy for them meant independence from both institutional politics (such as parties, unions, and state agencies) and male domination in different spheres of life, including squats and autonomist organizations (Gil 2011: 57); on the other hand, autonomy invited women to take matters into their own hands, to empower and liberate themselves by cooperating with each other and by establishing "networks of counter-power" (Gil 2011: 46).

The legacy of the 1960s and 1970s in terms of the politicization of private and personal matters (seclusion of family life, abortion, contraceptive methods, sexual freedom, domestic work, harassment and rape, etc.) paved the way for more ambitious concerns in the 1990s: rights for LGBTQIA people; opposition to militarism; the precarious labor of women, especially those making a living through sex work and domestic labor; immigration; and even feminist porn. These topics hardly recalled the attention of the more institutionalized branches of feminism but, in turn, found a fertile ground of expression in the squatted social centers and, above all, in the feminist squats (Gil 2011: 46, 68–97, 295– 298).

Conversely, this development questioned sexism, LGBTQIA-phobia, and racism within the squats and autonomist scenes. Furthermore, it revealed how neoliberal capitalism manipulates the notion of autonomy in order to promote free individuals to consume, vote, and comply. This is manifest in the so-called "crisis of care" for children, the elderly, the ill, the disabled, and its gendered and racialized dimensions. Self-determination and cooperation of the oppressed, thus, entail an essential inter-dependence with one another and a systemic (anti-capitalist, anti-patriarchal, and anti-racist) search for alternatives to the crisis of care, which is on the shoulders of women, in order to halt the reproduction of capitalism:

> Capitalism... has turned personal and collective autonomy upside down...: atomized experiences, competition with each other, self-entrepreneurialism... no future prospects... vertiginous rhythms of survival and production... fragile communities... loneliness.... The ideal of independence... [only applies to] personal and social situations in transit, casual ones, based on youth, health, strength, power, wealth, and without care for other people (their offspring, the elderly, the ill, etc.). (Gil 2011: 305)

Therefore, when individual autonomy is introduced in this approach, it is always defined together with issues of social interdependence and the constraints set in place by capitalist society.

Self-critical analyses within Spanish autonomist politics and squats are illuminating too; for example, the short-lived span of many organizations and squatting experiences, the superficial discussion of feminist concerns and the ineffective practices against sexism, the rejection of experts and professionals (except lawyers, to some extent) as well as accusations of vanguardism to the most devoted and politicized activists (Carretero 2012), to name just a few.

When the autonomist experience cross-fertilized the global justice movement in the late 1990s and early 2000s (Martínez 2007), other shortcomings were brought forward like multi-militancy, irreconcilable tensions with the institutional left, scarcity of resources, as well as a high diversity that resulted in the alter-globalization movement's fragmentation and a limited capacity for mass mobilization (Flesher 2007). Nevertheless, autonomists contributed to this larger protest wave (and to the 2011 upheavals [Flesher 2014]) with practical skills rooted in assembly-based organizations and with engagement in urban politics while bridging self-managed squatted buildings and more global issues. As Flesher writes:

> The autonomous actor actively attempts to negate the isolationism created by capitalist consumer society, through the nurturing of social relations that create community.... Just as single total identities (e.g. worker) do not make sense from an autonomous perspective, neither do single issues. (Flesher 2007: 340)

Although squatting was criminalized in 1995, the movement remained active in many cities over the following decades and even experienced a remarkable upsurge in the aftermath of the global financial crisis of 2008 (Martínez 2018). Since the 2000s, an explicit autonomist identity has been reshaped by networks of squatted and non-squatted social centers, especially those more inclined to legalize their spaces and to interact more directly with some public policies and state institutions—despite all the difficulties they faced—such as the Casa Invisible shows in Málaga (Toret et al. 2018).

A common theme of the so-called "second generation of social centres," shared with many Italian post-autonomists, was their intention to get rid of stereotyped identities and to engage with broader publics like neighborhoods social and political organizations, migrants, precarious workers, and artists. However, a diffused notion of autonomy quite intertwined with anarchism and a strong anti-institutional standpoint has to date prevailed among the squatters of Madrid, Barcelona, Valencia, Seville, and Zaragoza, for instance. The main turning point was represented by the emergence of a housing movement led by a formal organization called the PAH (Platform for People Affected by Mortgages) in 2009.

This movement also occupied buildings but rarely developed social centers. Many of their activists had an autonomist background and still endorsed it, but they mainly claimed affordable housing, the increase of social housing, and substantial changes in housing policies. Therefore, a more institutional approach was combined with the social empowerment of those who became homeless due to the widespread financialization of housing (Martínez 2019).

Conclusions

The term "autonomy" has been rightly criticized because it is charged with the burden of liberal and individualistic connotations, even when adopted by countercultural and anarchist trends (Bookchin 1998). As Flesher noted, "Although the legitimate political actor is the autonomous individual, acting collectively, this does not translate into a rejection of collectives or affinity groups." (Flesher 2007: 340) She also argues that organizations are dispensable for autonomists because they only "exist to serve the desires and goals of the individuals participating in them" (Flesher 2007: 339). Therefore, it is not uncommon to see individual subjectivity, autonomy, and independence as the pivotal bases of the autonomist political identity. This is explicit in widely circulated texts such as the *Temporary Autonomous Zone* (Bey 1985: 114) and pamphlets engaging with individualistic anarchism and the "radical criticism of any authority principle" (Mudu 2012: 414).

Some post-workerist and feminist activist-scholars also attached the language of desire and subjectivation to autonomy (Berardi 2016, Gil 2011: 100), although they always interpreted them according to broader social conflicts of domination in late capitalism, not as an individualistic approach to autonomy. Squatting movements following an autonomist orientation represented a practical way to refuse salaried labor and establish free spaces for the emancipation of women and LGBTQIA people. However, artistic squatters in France and Germany, for example (Aguilera 2018, Novy and Colomb 2013), have been frequently accused of adhering to the creative and individual view of autonomy rather than its more subversive, organized, prefigurative and collective forms of class struggle. Squatted social centers such as Tacheles in Berlin and Gängeviertel in Hamburg, for instance, would exemplify individual self-interests in "the seizing of cheap studio spaces" (Novy and Colomb 2013: 1828) and were instrumental to neoliberal city-branding policies aiming to attract well-educated but precarious creative classes. An additional feature that populates the distinctions between the autonomous and institutional Left refers to decision-making processes. Autonomists oppose delegation and most prefer face-to-face assemblies and consensus over voting (Piazza 2013). This implies that specific individuals may veto collective decisions or force the collective into long discussions, postpone agreements and even result in stalemates and internal splits. Notwithstanding these risks, the relatively small-scale size and the decentralization of autonomist networks posed no substantial threats to the persistence and predominance of consensual principles over time, although majority-rule voting has also been adopted by many squats.

In this article, I have argued that the meanings attached to autonomism by Italian, German, and Spanish squatters, in tight connection with the activists from intertwined movements, prompted me to prefer social autonomy in order to represent their novel contribution to urban politics. This approach reminds of 'social anarchism' or 'libertarian communism' in its aspiration to set up 'communities of equals' (Bookchin 1998; Graeber 2004: 2, 65–66). Nonetheless, autonomists go beyond anarcho-syndicalism, the factory walls, the central role of the working-class, and the Utopian models of a post-revolutionary future (Foucault 1982). They oppose all forms of domination spread throughout the metropolitan space by seeking cooperation with all oppressed social groups and by focusing pragmatically on the oppression they all experience at present. Therefore, emancipation is conceived as the political responsibility of the oppressed themselves. Instead of following vanguard leaders and external organizations, autonomists set direct democracy, assemblies, and horizontal cooperation at the top of their political agenda and practice. To fight the oppressors implies becoming separated from them and affirming the identity of the oppressed, temporarily, while the subordination and the resistance persist (Fraser 2008). Social autonomy thus indicates: (1) separation from the oppressors and the social relations where oppression occurs; (2) self-affirmation of the oppressed groups in direct social conflict with the oppressors; and (3) self-determination of the norms, decisions, and goals through the collective self-management of resources and spaces.

Their disbelief in future utopias and essentialist differences leads autonomists to attempt any possible revolution here and now. Thus, they aim to shape, in a prefigurative manner, spaces of equality, creativity, and resistance among those struggling together. As I argued above, the self-management and socio-political aggregation provided by squats (Piazza 2018) and other autonomous social centers (Hodkinson and Chatterton 2006) are the best materializations of autonomist politics. Illegal and disruptive means of protest, when targeting empty buildings, supply affordable spaces to those who wish, in turn, to separate themselves from patriarchal domination and the capitalist dynamics of labor exploitation, mass consumption, and urban speculation. Squats also provide safe and self-organized spaces for immigrants and refugees (Colectivo Hinundzurük 2018, Refugee Accommodation 2018). Buildings are rehabilitated, resources are shared, domestic life is often unfolded through collective decision-making, and the ethics of do-it-yourself (DIY) and do-it-together (DIT) is put in practice, counter-cultural expressions and radical left ideas are promoted, and other movements' activists and campaigns are hosted (Cattaneo et al. 2014, McKay 1998, Notes from Nowhere 2003, Van der Steen et al. 2014). Everyday life as the sphere of social reproduction, consisting of welfare services as well as the collective self-management of the buildings and urban areas where they live, has become a central concern for autonomism and squatting. As Federici explains, "the rediscovery of reproductive work has made it possible... to redefine the private sphere as a sphere of relations of production and a terrain of anticapitalist struggle" (Federici 2012: 97).

As a common thread shared by most autonomist and anarchist traditions, both state-driven socialism and capitalism (and, in its late stages, as global neoliberalism and financialization as well) are confronted. Autonomism is nurtured by a strong anti-authoritarian concern that seeks the experience of freedom in all spheres of social life, for all, and as immediately as possible. This entails the need for the oppressed to exert their available power and to use their own capacities in order to be released from the chains of domination, which can be designated as an immediatist struggle: "In such struggles," says Foucault, "people criticize instances of power which are the closest to them." (Foucault 1982: 780)

Not only are 'dictatorships of the proletariat' and one-party regimes resisted, but so too are all state institutions and formal organizations in liberal democracies that may reproduce social domination and inequality. Capitalism, patriarchy, racism, fascism, and imperialism are thus seen as notoriously resilient in both authoritarian and pluralist regimes, which determines the multiple points of bottom-up resistance and the corresponding autonomous struggles. Squatted spaces are manifestations of this micro-politics (Dadusc 2017, Yates 2014) of the 'everyday life' (Katsiaficas 2006) in small living and self-managed communities, domestic and small-group relations, as well as horizontal affinity groups. Squatters themselves also organize protest campaigns broadly and foster networks of solidarity with other autonomous and grassroots struggles worldwide (Mudu 2012).

My emphasis on the social features of autonomism also involves a long-lasting commitment to the struggles of women, LGBTQIA communities, migrants, and ethnic minorities. The feminist call to politicize, disclose, question, and abolish oppression in every sphere of private life pervades the internal spaces of squats, making them more open and public but with a broader anti-systemic stance. Despite being subject to forced temporality and nomadism, squatters who take over abandoned buildings usually aim to stay as long as possible. The persistence of squatters' movements also indicates the existence of networks that make them more challenging to the status quo than isolated activism and insurrectional uprisings. The autonomist ethos, regardless of being expressed through vague and diffuse political identities, radiates from the specific urban spots of the squats to the neighborhoods and other urban struggles intertwined with them, as far as coalitions are forged and are capable of articulating commonalities.

Nonetheless, autonomist projects are, more often than not, constrained and menaced by the political and economic conditions that surround them. On the one hand, state repression and maneuvers to institutionalize, integrate, and neutralize autonomous struggles severely reduce their radical reach and engender or accentuate splits among activists (Karpantschof and Mikkelsen 2014). Privatization and outsourcing of collective consumption by the state also hinder how squatted social centers relate to social needs, public services, and the market (Membretti 2007, Moroni and Aaster 1996). Frequently, urban activists need to break apart from the isolated *ghettos* of many autonomist and countercultural scenes, and connect with the society at large through institutional actors, professionals, and mass media (Castells 1983: 322) or use the resources of the institutional left (Flesher 2007: 345). On the other hand, the concern for everyday life implies a continuous warning about the reproduction of social dominations inside autonomous movements. Sexism is the most prominent and overtly debated one but is far from unique. Some of the major internal troubles infiltrating autonomist movements have been; tendencies towards dogmatism; retreating to individual and neoliberal forms of autonomy; alternative performances of vanguardism and hierarchy (Kadir 2016); exclusionary lifestyles and aesthetics

(Flesher 2007:350); exhaustion from long-lasting conditions of illegality; an excessive and unwanted fragmentation of politicized groups; as well as endless dissatisfaction with the political achievements of the struggles, due to their limited revolutionary capacity (Koopmans 1995). Both the above-mentioned achievements and the experienced problems of autonomism would thus deserve further investigation.

References

Aguilera, Thomas (2018) The Squatting Movement(s) in Paris: Internal Divides and Conditions for Survival. In Miguel A. Martínez (Ed.) *The Urban Politics of Squatters' Movements*. New York: Palgrave Macmillan, 121-144.

Aureli, Andrea and Pierpaolo Mudu (2018) Squatting: Reappropriating Democracy from the State. *Interface* 9(1): 497-521.

azozomox (2014) Squatting and Diversity: Gender and Patriarchy in Berlin, Madrid and Barcelona. In Claudio Cattaneo and Miguel Martínez (Eds.) *The Squatters' Movement in Europe. Commons and Autonomy as Alternatives to Capitalism*. London: Pluto, 189-210.

azozomox and Armin Kuhn (2018) The Cycles of Squatting in Berlin (1969-2016). In Miguel A. Martínez (Ed.) *The Urban Politics of Squatters' Movements*. New York: Palgrave Macmillan, 145-164.

Bailey, Ron (1973) *The Squatters*. Harmondsworth: Penguin.

Balestrini, Nanni and Primo Moroni (1997) [2006] *La horda de oro (1968- 1977). La gran ola revolucionaria y creativa, política y existencial*. Madrid: Traficantes de Sueños.

Berardi, Franco (Bifo) (2016) What is the Meaning of Autonomy Today? Subjectivation, Social Composition, Refusal of Work. *Multitudes*. http://www.multitudes.net/what-is-the-meaning-of-autonomy/

Bey, Hakim (1985) *The Temporary Autonomous Zone*. New York:Autonomedia.

Bhattacharya, T. (Ed.) (2017) *Social Reproduction Theory. Remapping Class, Recentering Oppression*. London: Pluto.

Bookchin, Murray (1998) *Social Anarchism or Lifestyle Anarchism: An Unbridgeable Chasm*. San Francisco: AK Press.

Carretero, José Luis (2012) La apuesta autónoma. In Salamanca, Francisco and Gonzalo Wilhelmi (Eds.) *Tomar y hacer en vez de pedir y esperar. Autonomía y movimientos sociales. Madrid 1985-2011*. Madrid: Solidaridad Obrera, 35-50.

Casanova, Gonzalo (2002) *Armarse sobre las ruinas. Historia del movimiento autónomo en Madrid (1995-1999)*. Madrid: Potencial Hardcore.

Castells, Manuel (1983) *The City and the Grassroots. A Cross-Cultural Theory of Urban Social Movements*. Berkeley: University of California Press.

Cattaneo, Claudio and Miguel Martínez (Eds.) (2014) *The Squatters' Movement in Europe: Commons and Autonomy as Alternatives to Capitalism,* London: Pluto.

Colectivo Hinundzurük (2018) You Can't Evict a Movement: From the Rise of the Refugee Movement in Germany to the Practice of Squatting. In SqEK (Ed.) *Fighting for Spaces, Fighting for our Lives: Squatting Movements Today.* Münster: Assemblage, 16-37.

Dadusc, Deanna (2017) *The Micropolitics of Criminalisation: Power, Resistance and the Amsterdam Squatting Movement.* Amsterdam: University of Kent [PhD Dissertation].

Debord, Guy (1967) *The Society of the Spectacle.* New York: Zone Books.

Della Porta, Donatella, and Dieter Rucht (1995) Left-libertarian Movements in Context: A Comparison of Italy and West Germany 1965–1990. In J. Craig Jenkins and Bert Klandermans (Eds.) *The Politics of Social Protest: Comparative Perspectives on States and Social Movements.* London: UCLPress, 229–273.

Della Porta, Donatella, and Gianni Piazza (2008) *Voices of the Valley. Voices of the Straits. How Protest Creates Communities.* New York: Berghahn.

Di Feliciantionio, Cesare (2017) Spaces of the Expelled as Spaces of the Urban Commons? Analysing the Re-emergence of Squatting Initiatives in Rome. *International Journal of Urban and Regional Research* DOI:10.1111/1468-2427.12513.

Estebaranz, Jtxo (2005) *Tropicales y Radicales. Experiencias alternativas y luchas autónomas en Euskal Herriak (1985-1990).* Bilbao: Likiniano Elkartea.

Federici, Sylvia. (2012) *Revolution at Point Zero. Housework, Reproduction, and Feminist Struggle.* Oakland: PM.

Feliciantonio, Cesare di (2017) Spaces of the Expelled as Spaces of the Urban Commons? Analysing the Re-emergence of Squatting Initiatives in Rome. *International Journal of Urban and Regional Research* 41(5): 708-725.

Finchett-Maddock, Lucy (2016) *Protest, Property and the Commons. Performances of Law and Resistance.* Abingdon: Routledge.

Flesher, Cristina (2007) Autonomous Movements and the Institutional Left: Two Approaches in Tension in Madrid's Anti-globalization Network. *South European Society and Politics* 12(3): 335-358.

Flesher, Cristina (2014) *Social Movements and Globalization: How Protests, Occupations and Uprisings are Changing the World.* New York: Palgrave Macmillan.

Flesher, Cristina, and Laurence Cox (Eds.) (2013) *Understanding European Movements: New Social Movements, Global Justice Struggles, Anti-Austerity Protest.* Abingdon: Routledge.

Foucault Michel (1982) The Subject and Power. *Critical Inquiry* 8(4): 777–795.

Fraser, Nancy (2008) *Adding Insult to Injury.* London: Verso.

Gaillard, Edith (2013) *Habiter autrement : des squats féministes en France et en Allemagne. Une remise en question de l'ordre social.* PhD Dissertation. Tours: François Rabelais University.

Geronimo (2012) *Fire and Flames. A History of the German Autonomist Movement.* Oakland: PM Press.

Gil, Silvia (2011) *Nuevos feminismos. Sentidos comunes en la dispersión.* Madrid: Traficantes de Sueños.

Graeber, David (2004) *Fragments of an Anarchist Anthropology.* Chicago: Prickly Paradigm.

Grazioli, Margherita and Caciagli, Carlotta (2018) Resisting the Neoliberal Urban Fabric: Housing Rights Movements and the Re-appropriation of the 'Right to the City' in Rome, Italy. *Voluntas* 29(4). https://doi.org/10.1007/s11266-018-9977-y

Hodkinson, Stuart and Paul Chatterton (2006) Autonomy in the City? Reflections on the Social Centres Movement in the UK. *City* 10: 305–315.

Holm, Andrej and Armin Kuhn (2011) Squatting and Urban Renewal: The Interaction of Squatter Movements and Strategies of Urban Restructuring in Berlin. *International Journal of Urban and Regional Research* 35(3): 644– 658.

Kadir, Nazima (2016) *The Autonomous Life? Paradoxes and Authority in the Squatters Movement in Amsterdam.* Manchester: Manchester University Press.

Karpantschof, René, and Flemming Mikkelsen (2014) Youth, Space, and Autonomy in Copenhagen: The Squatters' and Autonomous Movement, 1963- 2012. In Bart Van Der Steen, Ask Katzeef and Leendert Van Hoogenhuijze (eds.)*The City Is Ours. Squatting and Autonomous Movements in Europe from the1970s to the Present.* Oakland: PM, 179-205.

Katsiaficas, George (2006) *The Subversion of Politics: European Autonomous Social Movements and the Decolonization of Everyday Life.* Oakland: AK Press.

Knabb, Ken (1997) The Joy of Revolution. http://www.bopsecrets.org/PS/index.htm

Koopmans, Ruud (1995) *Democracy from Below. New Social Movements and the Political System in West Germany.* Boulder: Westview.

Maddanu, Simone (2018) The Theater as a Common Good: Artists, Activists and *Artivists* on Stage. *Interface* 10(1-2): 70-91.

Martin, John N. and Primo Moroni (2007) *La luna sotto casa. Milano tra rivolta esistenziale e movimenti politici.* Milan: ShaKe.

Martínez, Miguel A. (2007) The Squatters' Movement: Urban Counterculture and Alter-globalisation Dynamics. *South European Society and Politics* 12(3): 379– 398.

Martínez, Miguel A. (2013) The Squatters' Movement in Europe: A Durable Struggle for Social Autonomy in Urban Politics. *Antipode* 45(4): 866–887.

Martínez, Miguel A. (2018) Socio-Spatial Structures and Protest Cycles of Squatted Social Centres in Madrid. In Martínez, Miguel A. (Ed.) *The Urban Politics of Squatters' Movements*. New York: Palgrave Macmillan, 25-49.

Martínez, Miguel A. (Ed.) (2018) *The Urban Politics of Squatters' Movements*. New York: Palgrave Macmillan.

Martínez, Miguel A. (2019) Bitter Wins or a Long-distance Race? Social and Political Outcomes of the Spanish Housing Movement. *Housing Studies* 34(10): 1588-1611.

McKay, George (Ed.) (1998) *DiY Culture: Party and Protest in Nineties Britain*. London: Verso.

Mudu, Pierpaolo (2009) Where is Hardt and Negri's Multitude? Real Networks in Open Space. *ACME. An International E-Journal for Critical Geographies* 11(3): 211-244.

Mudu, Pierpaolo (2012) At the Intersection of Anarchists and Autonomists: Autogestioni and Centri Sociali. *ACME. An International E-Journal for Critical Geographies* 11(3): 413-438.

Mudu, Pierpaolo (2014) 'Ogni Sfratto Sarà una Barricata': Squatting for Housing and Social Conflict in Rome. In Cattaneo, Claudio and Miguel Martínez(Eds.) *The Squatters' Movement in Europe: Commons and Autonomy as Alternatives to Capitalism,* London: Pluto, 136-163.

Mudu, Pierpaolo, and Luisa Rossini (2018) Occupations of Housing and Social Centres in Rome: A Durable Resistance to Neoliberalism and Institutionalization. In Miguel Martínez (ed.) *The Urban Politics of Squatters' Movements*. New York: Palgrave Macmillan, 99-120.

Notes From Nowhere (2003) *We Are Everywhere: The Irresistible Rise of Global Anticapitalism*. London: Verso.

Owens, Lynn (2009). *Cracking under pressure. Narrating the decline of the Amsterdam squatters' movement*. Amsterdam: Amsterdam University Press.

Padrones, Sheila (2017) *El movimiento de okupación como proceso emancipador. El caso de Donostialdea*. PhD Thesis. Elche: Universidad Miguel Hernández.

Piazza, Gianni (2011) 'Locally Unwanted Land Use' Movements: the Role of Left- wing Parties and Groups in Trans-territorial Conflicts in Italy. *Modern Ital* 16(3), 329–344.

Piazza, Gianni (2013) How do Activists Make Decisions within Social Centres? InSqEK (Ed.) *Squatting in Europe. Radical Spaces, Urban Struggles*. Wivenhoe:Minor Compositions, 89-111.

Piazza, Gianni (2018) Squatting Social Centres in a Sicilian City: Liberated Spaces and Urban Protest Actors. *Antipode* 50(2), 498–522.

Pruijt, Hans (2013) The Logic of Urban Squatting. *International Journal of Urban and Regional Research* 37(1), 19–45.

Pruijt, Hans, and Conny Roggeband (2014) Autonomous and/o Institutional-ized Social Movements? Conceptual Clarification and Illustrative Cases. *International Journal of Comparative Sociology* 55(2): 144 –165.

Refugee Accommodation Space City Plaza (2018) Refugees' Struggles in Athens: Voices from City Plaza. In In SqEK (Ed.) *Fighting for Spaces, Fighting for our Lives: Squatting Movements Today*. Münster: Assemblage, 351-356.

Sadler, Simon (1998) *The Situationist City*. Cambridge: The MIT Press.

Salamanca, Francisco, and Gonzalo Wilhelmi (Eds.) (2012) *Tomar y hacer envez de pedir y esperar. Autonomía y movimientos sociales. Madrid 1985-2011*. Madrid: Solidaridad Obrera.

Seminario (2014) *Okupa Madrid (1985–2011). Memoria, reflexión, debate y auto-gestión colectiva del conocimiento*. Madrid: Diagonal.

Smart, Alan (2014) Provo. In Cattaneo, Claudio and Miguel Martínez (eds.) *The Squatters' Movement in Europe: Commons and Autonomy as Alternatives to Capitalism*, London: Pluto, 113.

Toret, Javier et al. (Eds.) (2008) *Autonomía y Metrópolis. Del movimiento okupa a los centros sociales de segunda generación*. Málaga: ULEX- Lainvisible.net- Diputación Provincial de Málaga.

Van Der Steen, Bart; Ask Katzeef, and Leendert Van Hoogenhuijze, L. (eds.) (2014) *The City Is Ours. Squatting and Autonomous Movements in Europe from the 1970s to the Present*. Oakland: PM.

Valli, Chiara (2015) When Cultural Workers Become an Urban Social Move-ment: Political Subjectification and Alternative Cultural Production in the Macao Movement, Milan. *Environment and Planning A* 47: 643–659.

Vasudevan, Alexander (2017) *The Autonomous City. A History of Urban Squat-ting*. London: Verso.

Ward, Colin, and David Goodway (2014) *Talking Anarchy*. Oakland: PM. Wen-nerhag, Magnus; Christian Fröhlich and Grzegorz Piotrowski (Eds.) (2018). *Radical Left Movements in Europe*. Abingdon: Routledge.

Yates, Luke (2014) Rethinking Prefiguration: Alternatives, Micropolitics and Goals in Social Movements. *Social Movement Studies: Journal of Social, Cultural and Political Protest* 14(1): 1-21.

Chapter 4

So Close and Yet So Far Apart:
Feminists, Autonomen, and Sexual Violence Within the Radical Left in Contemporary Germany

Émeline Fourment

Université de Rouen Normandie, France

In *The Subversion of Politics*, George Katsiaficas argues that "the women's movement prefigured what would later become the Autonomen" (1997, p. 103)[1]. Indeed, German feminists of the 1960s and 1970s were pioneers in the formulation of the ideal of autonomy, which was not only understood as a need for self-organization independent of men but also as a positioning against the state.[2] They created their own structures known as "counter-institutions," like squats, bars, and publications, which were organized according to anti-hierarchical principles. The most important element shared by Autonomen and feminists might be the politicization of the private. While feminists see sexuality, housework, or domestic violence as important political issues, Autonomen want to create "free spaces" where an everyday life free from oppression is possible. Both defend a counter-cultural vision of political action which implies fundamental transformations in the activist's way of life. However, despite these similarities, the relationship between feminists and Autonomen has been anything but fluid. The "continuing problem of sexism in the movement" (Katsiaficas, 1997, p. 239) led and still leads to numerous debates between leftist activists and feminists who were engaged in the Autonomen movement or are today engaged in the radical left. I would like to examine these debates in depth because I believe that they reveal much more than the internal contradictions of the Autonomen movement, as it is generally argued. They inform us above all about the way feminism and countercultural politics have been discussed within this movement.

It is difficult to overlook the numerous files on rape cases when examining the archives from the Autonomen.[3] These files provide evidence not only of the persistent problem of sexism in the movement but also of the crucial feminist presence naming sexism and sexual violence as issues to be addressed. The debates on rape—despite their persistence—have not been sufficiently discussed in scholarship on the Autonomen. In a recent book's contribution based on 32 interviews made in the 2010s with Autonomen who are critical with their past activism, Ali Jones (2018) concludes that these debates established a "lynch mob-type group mentality." She seems to accuse feminist Autonomen of using destructive violence against the community.[4] Her analysis reproduces most of the antifeminist stereotypes (Abbou, 2015; Blais et Dupuis-Déri, 2012; Devreux et Lamoureux, 2012; Gotell et Dutton, 2016) and does not take into account the literature on sexual violence and its mechanisms. Analyzing 350 articles of the Autonomen journal from Berlin, the *Interim*, Sebastian Haunss (2004) provides a much better insight into debates on rape within the Autonomen movement. According to him, the latter played a key role in the construction of the Autonomen collective identity: they participated in defining the (antisexist) boundaries of the Autonomen movement vis-à-vis the rest of the society (identified as sexist); they also shaped the most important lines of conflict within the movement (Haunss, 2004, p. 149-169). I agree with S. Haunss that debates on rape were crucial for the collective identity processes of the Autonomen. However, a focus on the movement's identity does not allow us to grasp all the dimensions of these debates. I worked extensively on the archives of some twenty rape accusations, which took place in several German towns and cities between 1984 and 2012. I also conducted field research in Göttingen and Berlin between 2013 and 2016.[5] While I was first interested in the analysis of gendered power relations within the Autonomen movement, I realized that these debates give us another perspective on the history of the Autonomen than the one developed in Katsiaficas's book *The Subversion of Politics*.

This contribution proposes to trace feminist mobilizations within the Autonomen movement through the debates on rape.

It analyzes these debates from the first years of the Autonomen movement until the movement's transformation into what is today called the "radical left."[6] I propose to thus expand our knowledge on the relationship between Autonomen and feminism and to contribute to the historiography of the German feminist movement.

I first focus on rape accusations occurring in the 1980s and 1990s and that have been characterized by the confrontational manner in which they were communicated by feminists. I show that these confrontational rape accusations must be analyzed (1) as the result of women's mobilization and (2) as opportunities to discuss sexism within the Autonomen movement. Then, (3) I analyze resistance to confrontational feminist action and show that they were firstly meant to maintain the status quo. Finally, I show that (4) feminists often disagreed with each other. These internal disagreements became so important at the turn of the 1990s that they provoked a change from confrontational to pedagogical modes of action.

Confrontational Rape Accusations as a Result of Women's Empowerment

Picture this: a wanted poster titled "Caution rapist!" with the full name of a man, his postal address, perhaps a photograph, and the name of his political group; graffiti on a house saying that a rapist lives there; a letter in an Autonomen newspaper naming a man accused of rape; slogans calling women to fight back—this is what accusations of rape looked like in the late 1980s and 1990s in the German Autonomen movement. Feminists defended this confrontational way of publicizing the perpetrators of sexual violence, saying that they wanted to let other women know that a certain man could be dangerous. According to them, this also justified publishing his full identity, so that the man could be recognized. But a deeper analysis shows that their confrontational accusations went beyond a protective function. By using a confrontational style, feminists wanted to reveal the existence of a "sex struggle" within the Autonomen movement. They were building two opposing camps: women and their allies in one camp, and enemies of women in the other. That is why we have to analyze rape accusations primarily as instances of women's mobilization, i.e., as feminist empowerment processes made possible by the founding of women's affinity groups.[7]

Women's Affinity Groups Facilitating Rape Accusations

Since sexual violence occurs in every sphere of society, it is not surprising that we find some cases in the Autonomen movement. What sets the Autonomen movement apart from other contexts where rape occurs is that women speak out against them and frame sexual violence in political terms. Political biographies of women in Autonomen movements show that most of them became feminists while active in the movement as a reaction to their comrades' sexism or violence and as a consequence of their encounters with experienced feminists in the movement. These women explain that they were regularly seen as potential girlfriends rather than as serious activists by Autonomen men, that their views were often ignored, and that their contributions to activism was not acknowledged.

According to these women, sexual violence crystallized all the dimensions of female subordination, reducing them to their body and denying what they said or wanted. These attitudes led to their informal exclusion from Autonomen activities and that is why many of them left and created their own WomenLesbians-only affinity groups (Dupuis-Deri, 2010).[8] The latter became essential for feminist politicization within the Autonomen movement (Schultze et Gross, 1997). In these spaces women could share their experiences of sexism, but they did not only focus on feminism. They participated in all Autonomen activities—like antifascist, anti-capitalist, and anti-imperialist actions—as WomenLesbians-only groups (Melzer, 2012). At the same time, they denounced the sexism of their comrades and thus struggled against men within the movement. The existence of these affinity groups has been a condition for victims of rape to speak out and that is why most of the rape accusations came from their members. Affinity groups thus provided places of support and solidarity for women, especially those who were survivors of sexual assault.

Rape Accusations as Instances of Women's Empowerment

While rape victims usually felt guilty and ashamed of what they had experienced, feminist affinity groups created a "new emotional common sense" (Gould, 2002), which made the transformation of shame into anger possible. Anger and rage were the first obvious characteristics of accusatory texts written by feminists in the 1980s and 1990s. Capital letters and several exclamation points gave the impression that feminists were yelling and screaming. Women turned these emotions into militant actions. They used violence as well in order to free themselves from it and make it visible. Thus, we can analyze confrontational rape accusations as sources of individual and collective empowerment.

First, they were instances of individual empowerment for the victim. She was not silenced anymore and the power dynamics shifted profoundly as the burden of shame attached to the aggressor by naming him publicly. She sometimes also confronted him verbally or physically. Some women even threw eggs or glue at their alleged rapists. Groups of women shouted at accused men in public spaces or (more rarely) beat them up. However, direct physical contact, which could put women in physical danger, remained in fact rare. The few instances that I found were related to cases of rape by a man who either was accused of a rape against a little girl (Wiltrud et al., 1991) or also locked up and tortured the woman.[9]

Nevertheless, this individual empowerment was only possible because of a strong solidarity among women: victims never acted alone. This way, rape accusations also implied collective empowerment. This is explicit in the way victims and their supporters presented themselves as fighters while claiming the political identity "women" by using the pronoun "we." Slogans like "We don't let violence against women happen without fighting back! We kick him out of our environments, our houses and our friendships, out of our events and bars!" communicated this collective empowerment (Die Frauen eines gemischten Zusammenhanges, 1992). Other slogans effectively called out to other women to join the cause, like "Women, be courageous and expose aggressors in public! Show solidarity to Women/Lesbians who are taking the risk to speak out in the public sphere! Women arm yourselves, fight back!" (nur mutig gelacht und zugebissen, 1995).

The assertion of a common political identity—"women" —underlined that sexual violence affects all women and that it is a reason why women should consider each rape as an attack against all of them and stand together. This construction of a woman's identity as a political tool is a characteristic of a radical feminist analysis. This one was in fact very widespread in Autonomen feminist circles in the 1980–90s and came along with an understanding of rape as the paroxysm of a continuum of violence and appropriation of women's bodies by men.

In other words, rape was not seen as a manifestation of an individual deviance or immorality but as an expression of male domination. The assertion of a woman's identity implied therefore that men were considered as the dominant group who benefited from women's oppression: in the sex struggle, they were the structural enemy of women. The slogan "all men are potential rapists" summarizes this politicization of sexual violence and is also recurrent in the texts that feminists published during debates on rape.

The adjective "potential" is important here because it underlines that the structural dominant position of men does not take away their agency. They can choose to participate actively in the domination or not; they can rape or not. Therefore, rape accusations offered the opportunity to reveal the sex struggle within the Autonomen movement: some men raped women, so feminists made that violence visible and responded to it with confrontational modes of action. In doing so, they both produced and revealed a line of division opposing women and their enemies and presented themselves as ready to fight. But the fact that debates on rape offered opportunities for feminists to speak about male domination within the Autonomen movement becomes more obvious when we look at the context in which these accusations were made.

Confrontational Rape Accusations as Opportunities to Speak About Sexism

When the first rapes were publicized in the 1980s, most Autonomen knew little, if anything, about feminism. Activists were against the oppression of women insofar as they were against all oppression, but they had not tackled the problem seriously. This changed in the 1990s due to feminist actions against sexual violence. That is why I argue that accusations of sexual violence have been a vehicle of a feminist consciousness not only for women but also for the whole movement.

Holding the Whole Movement Responsible

If we look at the way rapes were publicized in the 1980–90s, we notice that rape accusations never targeted the alleged rapist alone. They were addressed to the other members of the Autonomen movement too. This is very clear in the way the identity of accused men was published. In a movement which was partly based on collective housing, publishing the postal address of a perpetrator was also a way to expose a political community (the house); in addition, the name of his political group could also be mentioned if it was known.[10] Moreover, feminists held the whole Autonomen movement responsible for making sexual violence possible by tolerating sexism in everyday life. They especially targeted the other men who, though not rapists, demonstrated other sexist behaviors. This is explicitly expressed in the following text written by the support group for the victim of a case in 1989 Göttingen:

> The publication is also an expression of [the victim's] demand to [the rapist's, Klaus'] environment, friends and acquaintances to discuss the rape with Klaus, but also to deal with everyday, quite "normal" sexism of left-scene-guys who too often think they don't need to do it and do not question their own behavior. (No Name, 1989).[11]

The targeting of other activists was meant to hold them responsible for their behavior. In the 1989 Göttingen's debate quoted above, the victim did not, at first, demand their comrade to exclude Klaus. The victim wanted him, above all, to admit that he raped her. The question of exclusion came up in the following discussions. Nevertheless, in most cases, the demand for collective responsibility also implied a demand for an effective and definitive exclusion from Autonomen spaces. This type of demand could be interpreted as a will to punish the aggressor by ostracizing him. However, the question of punishment seems to have been marginal in feminist discussions. They saw exclusion much more as a way to reverse power relations between men and women. To accept that the aggressor remained in the movement would have in fact entailed excluding the victim. By contrast, to exclude him meant that the movement acknowledged the asymmetry of power between the victim (a woman) and the aggressor (a man) and thus favored the former. In the same way, feminists expected their comrades to always believe women who spoke out given the gendered power relations that usually kept them silent. Exclusion became therefore the symbol of recognizing patriarchy (Duriez, 2009). As emancipatory political action was seen as logically equivalent to being on the dominated side, feminists thus constructed equivalences between emancipatory political action and exclusion.

Rape Accusations Forced Autonomen to Speak about Sexism

These equivalences led to discussions with other Autonomen about the legitimacy of the feminist fight. Debates on rape dealt not only with concrete rape accusations, they were also abstract theoretical debates about patriarchy. We can find several political statements of Autonomen groups or individuals which reflect how they analyzed rape, patriarchy, and their connections to capitalism and imperialism. The following excerpt is a good example of this. It deals with a rape which was denounced in Bielefeld in 1987 and which was also discussed in other German cities such as Hamburg:

> Rape is absolutely racist violence, fascist subjugation of the woman in the imperialist class society. Like other forms of heavy class betrayal: brutal robbery, sadistic body injury, apolitical murder, denunciation...it exceeds a limit that cannot be offset with critique in our contexts. We do not deny the existence of socialization, brutalization and marketing of women as social conditions. Nevertheless, under the conditions of class society, we see no possibility to change this fundamental breach of any anti-systemic collectivity (Antifaschistiches Bündnis Hamburg, 1987).[12]

This excerpt is interesting for several reasons. First, the use of the adjective "racist" instead of "sexist" or "patriarchal" shows that these activists were not very familiar with feminist thought.[13] Second, their attempt to view rape through the lens of antifascism, anti-imperialism, and anticapitalism provides evidence of the prioritization of struggles: these activists needed to connect anti-patriarchy to their priority struggles in order to legitimize it. In fact, everything about the debate suggests that they were speaking about women's oppression for the first time on the occasion of this rape accusation. Yet, these activists were no exception.

Until the end of the 1980s, feminist Autonomen intervened in a context where women's struggles were not a topic of discussion for most of the male-dominated movement. By making rapes the topic of inevitable political debates of the Autonomen movement, they succeeded in imposing anti-sexism as a legitimate political issue. Sexual violence and feminism became so intricate that archive files on debates on rape are also referred to as "debates about sexism." Activists became sufficiently aware of feminist thought to argue against feminism using feminists' own terms. This feminist politicization did not happen without resistance. Most of the activists did not embrace the demand for exclusion, they criticized confrontational actions and questioned the relevance of radical feminist analysis.

Resistance to Confrontational Feminist Action

Demands of exclusion always encountered resistance. The feelings expressed in some of the contributions give us an idea of the atmosphere in the movement. While we saw that feminists were angry, their opponents were concerned about the potential destruction of the movement. This type of fear is not specific to Autonomen and can be observed in all relatively closed social groups like families, religious communities, and some professional environments (Neuburger, 2001). Rape accusations appear as a threat to the existence of the group because they uncover things which should not happen. In the case of families, they threaten the idea of the family's happiness. In the case of the Autonomen movement, they questioned its progressive identity and the activist camaraderie. In this context, feminists have faced two types of resistances. The first was a result of rape myths that circulated in the movement. The second challenged the equivalence made by feminists between exclusion and emancipatory political action.

Feminist Confrontational Action Facing Rape Myths

Researchers studying sexual violence define the "rape myth" as a set of representations of rape, its causes, consequences, perpetrators, and victims, that are commonly shared in a society (Davies et McCartney, 2003; Grubb et Turner, 2012; McMahon, 2010; Schwendinger et Schwendinger, 1974). Rape myths significantly differ from the social reality of rape and therefore contribute undermining and discrediting the victim's voice. Notably, they spread a false image of rapists as insane, poor, or perhaps part of a visible minority, when in fact they can be found in every social milieu. Another pervasive rape myth identifies the perpetrator as unknown to the victim, when in reality, the majority of rapes are committed by the victim's intimate partner or by a member of her family. Finally, it is erroneously assumed that most rapes occur in dark alleys, when in reality, they mostly take place at the victim's home (Müller, Schöttle, 2004).

In the context of the Autonomen movement, rape myths reinforced the idea that rapists could only be men outside of the movement. It was inconceivable for activists that their comrades and friends, with whom they fought for emancipation, could be capable of sexual violence. A woman was also often suspected of seeking revenge by making false accusations, especially if she had a relationship with the accused (as it was often the case). Thus, rape accusations have been either ignored or followed by public statements questioning or discrediting the victim. Some groups even organized informal trials, emulating the way state justice proceeds. They established a clear definition of sexual violence, heard the testimonies of the man and the woman and often concluded that the defendant was not guilty.[14]

In the 1980s, feminists participated in these debates defending their own point of view. Beginning in the 1990s, they systematically refused discussion arguing that there was nothing to discuss and that when a woman said she had been raped, it was the truth and could not be questioned. Confrontational modes of action thus became an accepted recourse for excluding rapists from the community. For instance, in 1999 a group of women attacked a bar called Schnarup Thumby in Berlin some days after a man accused of rape had been seen drinking a beer at one of the tables:

> We are tired of working with you! We will not discuss this anymore. We will act. That's why we, a group of WomenLesbians, attacked Schnarup Thumby on Tuesday evening,

7/27/1999. After throwing a pile of leaflets, we fired several shots with tear and pepper gas, deliberately aiming at the floor. (Schlagt-die-Sexisten-wo-ihr-sie-trefft-GmbH, 1999)

The fact that they attacked a bar and not only the accused man showed that their goal was not just to remove the man from Autonomen contexts, but to stress that his removal was due to a collective decision. It is also important to note that this type of direct action (with tear and pepper gas) was normally used against fascist bars. Moreover, the group's slogan, "Beat-sexists-where-you-meet-them-Ltd.," parodied the antifascist slogan, "Beat fascists where you meet them." This group of WomenLesbians consciously compared their comrades to fascists because they had not acted for the effective exclusion of the rapist. This is a good example of the way feminists could polarize the debate and thus draw a line between their supporters and everyone else.

Such confrontational actions and definite attitudes from feminists shifted the spotlight from the victim towards feminist groups. In all the debates, feminists quickly became the problem to be solved. Nevertheless, confrontation and refusing any discussion were the first feminist answer to rape myths.

Claiming a Pedagogical Approach to Maintain the Status Quo

The other type of resistance feminists faced was political criticism of their confrontational actions. This can be presented as two distinct types of criticism: the first focused on militancy, the second on the dividing line feminists had drawn between women and their enemies.

Militant direct action like the one described above always shocked other activists. Feminists were criticized for acting on emotions and for endangering the lives of their comrades. Even discursive militancy could become a topic of debate. This was the case in Berlin in 1999 when feminists used the slogans [both in English in the texts] "dead men can't rape" and "big sisters are watching you" for which they were accused by some Autonomen of defending the death penalty, reactionary security policies, and feudal justice. Some activists became paranoid, arguing that feminists were acting for intelligence services or fascist groups in order to destroy the Autonomen movement. This panic that feminist militancy provoked is surprising considering that the same types of actions or slogans were considered legitimate as long as they targeted fascists, the police, or the state.

The second type of criticism was more subtle. It recognized that sexual violence was a problem but criticized the equivalence feminists made between exclusion and emancipatory political action. While feminists were little interested in the rapist's fate and much more in the recognition of the incompatibility between sexual violence and emancipatory political action, this criticism put aggressors back in the spotlight. The argument created a division between an individual-centered pedagogical approach and a confrontational one. From the emancipatory perspective espoused by the pedagogical approach, the Autonomen had to acknowledge the human capacity to learn from mistakes.

According to this logic, rather than repressing and excluding aggressors, Autonomen were obligated to provide rapists with the opportunity to confront their past violent behavior in order to avoid repeating them. Through this redefinition of emancipatory political action, these activists also rejected the idea of a sex struggle. Because it held that a man could learn not to be sexist and violent, their approach contradicted the idea of a class enemy. They often refused to speak about victims as women and about rapists as men. Feminists, on the other hand, strongly argued against a pedagogical approach with the rapist, asserting that patriarchy could not been treated like a psychological illness and that rapists were the enemy of emancipatory political action just like Nazis or police.[15] This line of argument led supporters of the pedagogical approach to respond by criticizing feminists for polarizing the debate, thereby inhibiting communication. This was for instance asserted by the Antifascist Action Berlin (AAB) during a debate in 1999:

> A polarization between "the good comrades" and "the bad comrades" is suggested. A real discussion is thus averted. Instead, everyone tries to position himself on the "good side," and lip service thwarts the discussion about contradictions (AAB, 2000).

It is important to consider the context in which this argument was formulated by the AAB. In this case, the accused man belonged to the AAB. The accusation was made in January 1999, directly naming the AAB, and thus asking the group to ban the accused. The AAB reacted in March with a short text without positioning itself clearly. A few months later, the alleged rapist was seen at the Schnarup-Thumby bar which led to the above-mentioned feminist direct action. The AAB did not participate in the following debates. Thus, when they published a long text in January 2000, they did it to defend their decision not to exclude the aggressor because other activists called on them to explain their position.

In spite of this context, their text did not mention the specific circumstances surrounding the case in question, but rather criticized the way debates on rape occurred in the Autonomen movement. It also proposed another solution which would ensure the objectivity of decisions in cases of rape accusation. This solution was very similar to the organization of a trial. In this text, they also strongly argued for a pedagogical approach without clarifying precisely what such an approach would look like or entail. According to the archives I found, they themselves did nothing to "re-educate" or "reform" the member accused of rape. In this context, the argument in favor of pedagogy seems to have been a discursive and strategic way to avoid excluding their member. Yet, activists of the AAB were not the only ones who claimed a pedagogical approach to maintain the status quo in the 1980–90s. In fact, this happened so often that one might conclude that the pedagogical approach began as a way to avoid the politicization of sexual violence in the Autonomen movement. This situation changed at the turn of the twenty-first century.

From Antifeminist Criticism to Feminist Discourse: How Feminists Came to Pedagogy

In this section, I will first try to understand how feminists came to a pedagogical approach and then look at its implementation. Feminists began to develop a pedagogical approach in the 2000s not because they were suddenly convinced of their opponents' arguments but because feminism was undergoing a sea-change in Germany. Notably, the influence of deconstructivism seems to have been dramatic for WomenLesbian groups which almost all disappeared at the end of the 1990s. This change coincided with a growing feminist Autonomen interest for a pedagogical approach in case of rape accusation. This is very clear when we look further at the debate of 1999–2000 in Berlin.

After the AAB publicized its above cited text on "new objectivity," the focus of the debate shifted. Most of the published contributions were written by feminists and several of them were rather abstract and technical, citing academic sources. These texts give us important information about disagreements between feminists at the time of a reconfiguration of their movement. I would like to present two of them.

The first one is an elaborate justification of the exclusion of rapists against the "illusion" of a pedagogical approach. It replied to all the points of criticism which had been made against feminist confrontational actions, but it did so in general terms. The authors positioned themselves as experts: they provided a general analysis of the way rape accusations are discussed in the movement and explained why opponents of radical feminists are wrong, citing academic articles from the feminist research on sexual violence. For instance, they justify the need to believe women who speak out in this way:

> Central to the experience of violence is the personal feeling of transgression of limits, dispossession of the body and soul, curtailment of personality, until there remains only a torso that fits the norms set by men. (Kaveman 1989, 76). Due to this situation, the involved WomenLesbians must have the exclusive power to define a rape. (Eine FrauenLesben-Gruppe aus Berlin, 2000)

While in the name of objectivity one of the main points of the AAB text questioned the relevance of giving women alone the right to define what they experienced, these feminists answered with scientific arguments in order to legitimize their position. Using an American academic quoting style, they reinforced their point. By importing academic norms into an Autonomen debate, they mobilized the symbolic capital of the university and thus placed themselves in a position of authority. At the end of the 1990s, when gender studies were first being established at German universities, they became a resource for feminist students who were also involved in the Autonomen movement. Yet feminist research has never been homogeneous. Especially in Germany, the reception of *Gender Trouble* by

Judith Butler in 1990 provoked huge debates on constructivism (Hark, 2005; Möser, 2013; Purtschert, 2008). This heterogeneity has also been reflected in the debate on rape of 1999–2000. A few months later another feminist text was published beginning with these words:

> In the anniversary issue of the *Interim 500* "A WomenLesbians group from Berlin" wrote a contribution "on the way gender-mixed political contexts deal with rape." The quotations cited in the article are almost entirely from 1989 and clearly show the state of the discussion in the radical left. (Meiser, 2000)[16]

The authors of the text, Franz and Mandy Meiser,[17] presented themselves at the forefront of feminist research and used an evolutionist argument to discredit the text of "A WomenLesbians group from Berlin" which they saw as backward. Here we find a narrative which has appeared in some gender studies handbooks in Germany since the end of the 1990s. Feminist theory was headed for a dead-end in the 1980s, but recovered thanks to the reception of Judith Butler; deconstructivist feminist perspectives were thus synonymous with progress (Möser, 2013, p. 156).

In their following argument, Franz and Mandy Meiser explicitly argued for "deconstructivist ideas" against "black and white victim/aggressor analysis." However, they emphasized their feminist approach and distanced themselves from anti-feminist resistances. They were not against the exclusion of rapists but argued in favor of communicative processes between the woman and the man, with the support of other activists if needed, in order to determine if the man actually intended to rape. The authors based their argument on the idea of "grey zones":

> It always comes to situations where first the sex is ok and suddenly, for some reason, it is over. She cannot express it. He apparently does not notice anything. Hours, days or weeks later, there is a bad taste of the night. She feels raped by him; he could have known what was going on with her. He did not care, he just wanted his orgasm and for him it was a great night. She feels rightly raped. Is he therefore a rapist? (Meiser, 2000)

Introducing the idea that there were many situations which were neither rape nor consensual sex (i.e., grey zones), this contribution initiated a feminist debate on men's intention to rape which has been a condition for the development of a feminist pedagogical approach. As we saw, the confrontational approach considered that men choose deliberately to rape. The pedagogical approach questioned this idea. It considered that aggressors were often not conscious that they raped because of their patriarchal male socialization which did not teach them to consider women's consent. Rape was not only normalized in a patriarchal society, but it was also encouraged by normative patterns which assigned men and women respectively to active and passive sexual roles, they argued. Moreover, according to this idea, female socialization did not teach women to express their will. Therefore, in the case of unintended rape, miscommunication appeared to be the main cause of sexual violence. This point of view prefigures the approaches and tools feminists implemented in the 2000s and 2010s.

The Implementation of Feminist Pedagogical Approaches and its Obstacles

The pedagogical approaches developed by feminists in the new millennium differ from the ones defended in the 1980s and 1990s. Rather than focusing on accused men alone (i.e., the individualist approach), they are meant to make the whole movement responsible for consensual sex (i.e., a collectivist approach). This implies working to prevent sexual violence and implementing transformative justice processes when such violence occurs.

The first feminist pedagogical practices were developed in a context of growing expertise on sexual violence within the radical left. This expertise mobilized academic knowledge but also built on the sharing of experiences of leftist feminists. Although the WomenLesbians movement had disappeared, feminists continued to organize meetings, which gathered activists from all over Germany and dealt with sexual violence. This was the case with the "antisexist practices conferences" that took place six times between 2007 and 2014 in Berlin and whose main theme was sexual violence in political contexts. Moreover, several texts and even books have been published on this theme (like definitionsmacht.tk, 2007; Desesperados, 2006; GAP, 2007; re.ACTION, 2007; Wiesental, 2017).

Specialized groups were created to organize workshops about consent and about the way activists should react to rape accusations. These texts and workshops were used as pedagogical tools which allowed feminists to explain their views and discuss them. However, they were often presented from a position of authority which belongs to the pedagogical approach: feminists were the experts on the subject, and they passed their knowledge on. In this way, sexual violence became a technical subject which required specific knowledge. At the same time, confrontational modes of action almost disappeared.

These workshops and texts were meant to sensitize other activists about sexual violence. Some of them proposed the transformation of sexual practices through the lens of consent and communication. They asked the following questions: How can we express our will and desire? How can we ask when we are not sure our partner is enjoying what we do? How can consent become sexy? The related discussions proposed to free sexuality from taboo, to experiment with other ways of having sex and communicating about it.

Other workshops and texts dealt instead with sexual violence. They provided lists of good practices and methods of implementation. In such workshops, the feminist position of authority was often stronger than in workshops dedicated to sexuality in general. These workshops could also deal with transformative processes of justice which were the second type of practice that the feminist pedagogical approach developed.

Reflections on transformative justice appeared in Germany, especially in Berlin, at the end of the 2000s. Like activists in Montreal (Ingenito et Pagé, 2017), they borrowed from texts by North-American feminists of color, and put the question of justice at the center of the debate (which had not been the case of the previous Autonomen feminist discussion in Germany).[18] Given that racism makes incarceration of men of color much easier than the incarceration of white men, North-American feminists of color developed an alternative justice system, which was meant not to put more men of color in jail, but would still eliminate sexual violence from the community.

Their view of justice was thus a collective one which held communities partially responsible for sexual violence, because they prop up structures that make it possible. This view required preventative measures just like those that the feminists of the radical Left developed, but it also implied that pedagogical work with the rapist was necessary. These feminists did not see prison or exclusion as a way to protect women from sexual violence. They believed that men must unlearn sexual aggression, and they emphasized the community's role in helping them transform.

In Germany, several feminists have supported this view and tried to implement it. For example, in Berlin a transformative process began in 2012 when a man was accused of sexually assaulting a friend.[19] He was known to be especially violent when drinking and had assaulted women in the past. He agreed to enter a transformative process, which lasted three years. Three different groups were involved: a support-group for the victim, a transformative group that worked with the aggressor, and a supervision group that mediated between the two. The aggressor agreed to actively take part in the transformative work by being present at the meeting, trying to change his behavior, taking responsibility for his actions, and not assaulting anymore. He also agreed to quit drinking and to refrain from entering antisexist and feminist spaces until the end of the process (Anonymous, 2015). However, like many transformative processes, this one was unsuccessful, as not only did the aggressor fail to actively engage in the collective work, but his friend also failed to encourage him. It seems that the most important obstacle to the feminist pedagogical approach remains the failure by many to recognize that sexual violence is a serious political problem, and that pedagogy is not more effective than confrontational actions when the goal is honour the experiences of victims.

Conclusion

This contribution showed that debates about rape were a vehicle of a feminist politicization in the Autonomen movement throughout the 1980s and 1990s. They have led a lot of women to come together in affinity groups to expose sexual violence as a legitimate political issue and have enabled them to make sexual violence and feminism an unavoidable topic of Autonomen's political debates. I also demonstrated that the feminist politicization of the Autonomen movement has been heterogeneous and that feminist Autonomen's discussions on sexual violence reflected larger theoretical feminist discussions. Notably, the reception of deconstructivist perspectives constituted a basis for a feminist critique of confrontational actions and a claim for a pedagogical approach. Nowadays, confrontational actions have almost disappeared from the repertoire of the German feminist radical Left. Moreover, contemporary groups are less likely to advocate for the definitive exclusion of convicted rapists. The development of an expertise on sexual violence, informative workshops, and processes of transformative justice seems to have replaced these confrontational actions.

Whether they defend confrontational or pedagogical actions, feminist Autonomen have pointed out a recurring contradiction of autonomous projects: that establishing "alternative human lifestyles right now" within a society structured by power relations is a perilous exercise (Katsiaficas, 1997, p. 21). At first glance, denunciations of sexual violence seem to expose a failure of autonomous politics: they show that Autonomen did not manage to create an everyday life free from oppression. However, paradoxically, the study of feminist action reveals that rape publicizations are motivated by a feminist desire to deepen the realization of autonomy. This is evidenced by the feminists' refusal to resort to state justice. The political entity they call on is not the state but the Autonomen movement itself. In this way, these feminists demonstrate their will to stay away from state institutions and to place the struggle against sexual violence within the framework of autonomous politics.

The anger over the rape they denounce does not stop them believing in the movement and in its ability to recover from such ordeal. In this context, the various feminist debates on the emancipatory character of a mode of action appear as an attempt not only to restore, but also to deepen the realization of autonomy. Tracing the history of the autonomous movement through the history of debates on sexual violence highlights that autonomy is never acquired and is always an ongoing process.

Endnotes

1 I thank Yasemin Ural, Irina Mützelburg and Riley Ertel for their comments and language revisions.

2 I speak mostly about West Germany, even after 1989.

3 They are preserved in Autonomen spaces and self-managed by activists. I have been in the *"Juzi"* [*Jugendzentrum*; young center] in Göttingen and in the *Papiertiger Archiv* in Berlin.

4 A. Jones also compares feminist Autonomen's action against sexual violence to the crimes of Nazis against Jews (Jones, 2018, p. 152).

5 This research raised several methodological issues which I address in my PhD Thesis (Fourment, 2021). First, as Catherine Eschle (2018) shows, debates on sexual violence can cause disengagement. This is especially true for the Autonomen and it explains many difficulties in meeting feminists who were committed to the struggle against sexual violence within the Autonomen movement. Most of these activists had disappeared or did not want to discuss this issue because it brought back bad memories. It was much easier to meet activists who had been against these feminists. Second, these debates question the position of researchers in relation to the one of judges. It is not the researcher's job to say whether there has been rape. However, I choose to take Autonomen seriously. If these activists considered and still consider it important to have debates on rape, I consider that it was, and still is, a real problem for them. Moreover, this article focuses on feminist action and takes into account the research carried out on sexual violence, which in turn adds value to the statements of feminists.

6 Only the activists who were active in the 1980s or 1990s define themselves as Autonomen. Some younger activists say they are "post-Autonomen" but the majority just define themselves as part of the "radical Left." Nevertheless, these activists share a political ideal, which can still be called "autonomy," namely, independence from political parties, a counter-cultural view of political action and a radical critique of oppressions and hierarchies. Moreover, we can observe a strong continuity in the way accusations of sexism and sexual violence have been discussed in the movement from the 1980s until today.

7 The concept of "sex struggle" refers to a feminist approach which borrows the concept of class from anticapitalism while considering patriarchal oppression as independent from capitalist oppression. Similarly, to the class struggle, the sex struggle opposes two classes (men and women) who have antagonistic interests. The liberation of the dominated class (women) implies a dissolution of all classes which means the disappearance of genitals as socio-hierarchical criteria. This understanding of patriarchy and women's liberation has been well developed by Christine Delphy (2013) and was also a feature of US radical feminism. In the 1990s, some Autonomen feminists also spoke of a "sex war" [*Geschlechterkrieg*].

8 In the 1980-90s, feminists specified that their groups were only for "Women-Lesbians" [*FrauenLesben*] in order to make visible the presence of lesbians. This did not mean that all the women in their groups were lesbians.

9 See the debate in Hamburg in 1985 or the debate in Köln in 1986.

10 This has been the case for the Volksfront in 1987 in Bielefeld, for the Antifa M in 1995 in Göttingen and the Antifascist Action Berlin in 1999. The last two groups were part of the network Antifascist Action / Organized Nationwide (AA/BO).

11 Note that the support group speaks only about men's behavior and not about women who might support rapists. This is a common feature of the accusation of this time: women were called to solidarity and never attacked. While all men might be rapists, all women were expected to be allies.

12 The group declared then being in favor of the exclusion.

13 The use of the word "racism" to speak about sexism appears several times in the debate on the Bielefeld case to criticize oppression on the basis of biological characteristics. This also implies a definition of racism as biological determinism.

14 This is how several groups of the AA/BO proceeded. See especially the cases of 1995 in Göttingen and of 1999/2000 in Berlin.

15 Some pro-feminist men attempted to implement "radical therapy" to re-educate rapists at the end of the 1980s and beginning of the 1990s. These attempts seem to have mostly failed and thus provided feminists with even more evidence against the pedagogical approach.

16 No important text on the subject has been published since.

17 These are pseudonyms. It is interesting to note that the authors chose both male and female names—although they define themselves as feminists, they do not claim female identity.

18 The work of *Incite! Women of Color Against Violence* is the major reference. See: http://www.incite-national.org/.

19 See this website in particular: https://www.transformativejustice.eu/ [15.02.2018].

References

AAB. Antifaschistische Aktion Berlin [Antifascist Action Berlin] (2000, January). Neue Sachlichkeit. Beitrag zur Diskussion um Sexismus. [New objectivity. Contribution to the discussion on sexism] *Interim* 493 (Berlin).

Abbou, J. (2015). Des hyènes galeuses et agressives à la bouche écumante. Une analyse rhétorique de l'antiféminisme pamphlétaire. In F. Dupuis-Déri et D. Lamoureux (dir.), *Les antiféminismes. Analyse d'un discours réactionnaire* (p. 37-54). Remue-Ménage. Récupéré de https://hal.archives-ouvertes.fr/hal-01382816

Antifaschistiches Bündnis Hamburg [Antifascist Alliance Hamburg], G. (1987, April). *Wie gehen wir mit Vergewaltigung in revolutionären Zusammenhängen um?*

Blais, M. et Dupuis-Déri, F. (2012). Masculinism and the Antifeminist Counter-movement. *Social Movement Studies, 11*(1), 21-39.

Davies, M. et McCartney, S. (2003). Effects of gender and sexuality on judgements of victim blame and rape myth acceptance in a depicted male rape. *Journal of Community & Applied Social Psychology, 13*(5), 391-398.

definitionsmacht.tk. [right to define.tk] (2007). when my anger starts to cry... Debatten zur Definitionsmacht und der Versuch einer notwendigen Antwort [when my anger starts to cry... Debates about the right to define and the attempt of a necessary response]. *AS.ISM. Reader des Antisexismusbündnisses Berlin,* (2), 32-37.

Delphy, C. (2013). *L'ennemi principal.* Paris : Éditions Syllepse.

Desesperados, B. (2006). Über Definitionsmacht. Überarbeiteter Auszug aus dem Text « Antisexistische Basisbanalitäten » [About the right of definition. A revised excerpt from the text „antisexist basic banality]. *AS.ISM. Reader des Antisexismusbündnisses Berlin,* (1), 9-14.

Devreux, A.-M. et Lamoureux, D. (2012). *Cahiers du Genre. Les antiféminismes.* Paris, France: L'Harmattan, 2012.

Die Frauen eines gemischten Zusammenhanges [The women of a gender-mixed context]. (1992, December). weisste was, wir ham auch hass!! [you know what, we are also angry!!] *Amazora* 40, 39-40.

Dupuis-Deri, F. (2010). Anarchism and the Politics of Affinity Groups. *Anarchist Studies, 18*(1), 40-62.

Duriez, H. (2009). Chapitre 6 / Des féministes chez les libertaires remue-ménage dans le foyer anarchiste. In O. Fillieule et P. Roux (dir.), *Le sexe du militantisme* (p. 167-186). Paris: Presses de Sciences Po.

Eine FrauenLesben-Gruppe aus Berlin [A WomenLesbian group from Berlin]. (2000, April). Zur Umgehensweise mit Vergewaltigung in gemischtgeschlechtlichen politischen Zusammenhängen [About the way we deal with rape in gender-mixed political contexts]. *Interim* 500 (Berlin).

Eschle, C. (2018). Troubling stories of the end of occupy: Feminist narratives of betrayal at occupy Glasgow. *Social Movement Studies, 17*(5), 524-540.

Fourment, E. (2021). *Théories en action. Appropriations des théories féministes en milieu libertaire à Berlin et Montréal* (PhD Thesis in political science). Sciences Po Paris.

GAP. (2007). Was tun wenn's brännt. Zum Umgang mit sexueller Gewalt [What's to be done when it's buurning. About the way we deal with sexual violence] *AS.ISM. Reader des Antisexismusbündnisses Berlin,* (2), 26-30.

Gotell, L. et Dutton, E. (2016). Sexual Violence in the 'Manosphere': Antifeminist Men's Rights Discourses on Rape. *International Journal for Crime, Justice and Social Democracy, 5*(2), 65-80.

Gould, D. (2002). Life During Wartime: Emotions and the Development of Act Up. *Mobilization: An International Quarterly, 7*(2), 177-200.

Grubb, A. et Turner, E. (2012). Attribution of Blame in Rape Cases: A Review of the Impact of Rape Myth Acceptance, Gender Role Conformity and Substance Use on Victim Blaming. *Aggression and Violent Behavior, 17*(5), 443-452.

Hark, S. (2005). *Dissidente Partizipation: eine Diskursgeschichte des Feminismus.* Frankfurt-am-Main: Suhrkamp.

Haunss, S. (2004). *Identität in Bewegung: Prozesse kollektiver Identität bei den Autonomen und in der Schwulenbewegung.* Wiesbaden : Verlag für Sozial-wissenschaften.

Ingenito, L. et Pagé, G. (2017). Entre justice pour les victimes et transforma-tion des communautés : des alternatives à la police qui épuisent les féministes. *Mouvements, 4*(92), 61-75.

Jones, A. (2018). Anti, Anti, Anti! Counterviolence and Anti-sexism in Ham-burg's Autonomous Rote Flora Culture Centre. In S. Colvin et K. Karcher (dir.), *Gender, Emancipation, and Political Violence: Rethinking the Legacy of 1968* (p. 142-157). Abingdon, New York: Routledge.

Katsiaficas, G. N. (1997). *The Subversion of Politics: European Autonomous Social Movements and the Decolonization of Everyday Life.* Atlantic Highlands, N.J: Humanities Press.

McMahon, S. (2010). Rape Myth Beliefs and Bystander Attitudes Among In-coming College Students. *Journal of American College Health, 59*(1), 3-11.

Meiser, F. und M. (2000, September). Let's Take a Walk on the Wild Side. *Interim.*

Melzer, P. (2012). Frauen gegen Imperialismus und Patriarchat zerschlagen den Herrschaftsapparat": autonome Frauen, linksradikaler femin-istischer Protest und Gewalt in Westdeutschland. In *All we ever wanted...'eine Kulturgeschichte europäischer Protestbewegungen der 1980er Jahre,* (p. 157-177). Berlin : Dietz.

Möser, C. (2013). *Féminismes en traductions : théories voyageuses et traductions culturelles.* Paris : EAC, Éditions des Archives contemporaines.

Müller, U., Schöttle, M. (2004) *Lebenssituation, Sicherheit und Gesundheit von Frauen in Deutschland. Eine repräsentative Untersuchung zu Gewalt gegen Frauen in Deutschland.* Bundesministerium für Familie, Senioren, Frauen und Jugend.

Neuburger, R. (2001). Violences sexuelles intra-familiales. *Therapie Familiale, Vol. 22*(1), 39-50.

No Name. (2015). *Not my comrades. Ein Zine über Täterschutz, Solidarität, WERTschätzung & Unterstützung* [Not my comrade. A zine about protec-tion of aggressors, solidarity, esteem and support]. From https://notmy-comrade.noblogs.org/

No Name. (1989). *Rape accusation letter.*

nur mutig gelacht und zugebissen [only bravely laughed and bitten]. (1995, May). Redebeitrag am 20. Mai 95 [Speech on a demonstration on the 20th May 1995]. *Göttinger Drucksache* 192.

Purtschert, P. (2008). Des réactions troublantes : la réception de trouble dans le genre de Judith Butler dans le monde germanophone. *Sociétés contemporaines, n° 71*(3), 29-47.

re.ACTION, R. für emanzipatorische A. (2007). *Antisexismus_reloaded. Zum Umgang mit sexualisierter Gewalt. Ein Handbuch für die antisexistische Praxis* [Antisexism reloaded. About the way we deal with sexualized violence. A handbook for antisexist practice]. Münster : Unrast Verlag.

Schlagt-die-Sexisten-wo-ihr-sie-trefft-GmbH. (1999, July). Antifa heisst mit Vergewaltigern saufen ?! [Does Antifa mean to get drunk with rapists?!] *Interim* 482 (Berlin).

Schultze, T. et Gross, A. (1997). *Die Autonomen: Ursprünge, Entwicklung und Profil der autonomen.* Hamburg: Konkret Literatur.

Schwendinger, J. R. et Schwendinger, H. (1974). Rape Myths: In Legal, Theoretical, and Everyday Practice. *Crime and Social Justice,* (1), 18-26.

Wiesental, A. (2017). *Antisexistische Awarness. Ein Handbuch.* Münster: Unrast Verlag.

Wiltrud, Waltrud et Gertrud. (1991, August). Wir haben einen erwischt - wir erwischen euch alle !!! [We caught him - We will catch you all !!!] *Amazora* 21, 5-15.

Chapter 5

Designing Collective Autonomy:
Dimensions of the Anti-Authoritarian Political Project in Quebec

Rachel Sarrasin
Cégep Gérald-Godin and Collège
de Bois-de-Boulogne, Canada

As many observers have noted, one of the defining features of social movements that have emerged in contemporary waves of protest such as the Global Justice Movement or the more recent Indignados and Occupy events around the world is the presence of autonomous forms of resistance (Epstein 2001; Gordon 2002; Castells 2005; Graeber 2002; 2006; Day 2005; Luck 2008; Milstein 2010; Sarrasin et al. 2012; Glasius and Pleyers 2013; Ibáñez 2014; Dixon 2014; Ancelovici 2016). In spite of local variations and a diversity of denominations, these forms of resistance share common attributes with autonomous politics as documented by George Katsiaficas (1997, 2006), as they call "for power to the people and decentralization of decision-making" (Katsiaficas 2001: 547).[1] As he noted in his contribution to the topic, autonomous movements mark a turn away from "established political parties and trade unions" as well as from "traditional notions of revolutionaries," rather collectively privileging an organizational model "operated according to self-managed consensus, making decisions independently of central leaders and implementing them according to their own self-discipline" (Katsiaficas 2001: 548).

From a political analysis standpoint, autonomous movements raise interesting questions about the nature of power and the source of social change, as they refer to modes of organization and action that aim to be independent from existing state and market structures. Following this observation, autonomous forms of resistance are often located in the blind spot of the dominant political science paradigm which locates the prime site of political action in our interactions with the state. Therefore, autonomous movements are often perceived as resting outside of the political sphere because of their development in parallel to state institutions, the latter being considered as the legitimate power holders in society.

On the other hand, understandings of autonomous politics have also been framed by debates within social movements and left-wing activist circles that tend to oppose political strategies targeting state reforms versus those that aim for radical political change. This last debate has sometimes led to a normative perception of autonomous movements as betraying their original commitment to collective autonomy if ever they chose to strategically interact with conventional political actors in a given campaign, following their stance for a diversity of tactics.

This chapter reflects on how to bypass these dead ends in our ways of addressing autonomous politics, in order to fully grasp the nuances of collective autonomy as it unfolds over time. In short, collective autonomy as a goal can hardly be achieved overnight and it cannot completely evade mainstream institutions and actors. Indeed, although autonomous forms of resistance ultimately aim to break away from a statist and capitalist logic, they develop, at the same time, in a given institutional context that is framed by dominant actors. In order to problematize "the coordinates of the debate" (Dinerstein 2015: 8) regarding our understanding of contemporary autonomous movements, this chapter argues that collective autonomy, while being a political goal in itself, can also be deconstructed as an ongoing process designed by a variety of actors and practices.

This argument draws on autonomous politics as they have been developed by the anti-authoritarian community in the province of Quebec, mainly in Montreal, since 2000. Activists involved in this community share a common goal based on collective autonomy, advocating for practices promoting self-determination and self-organization, privileging direct democracy, direct action tactics and do-it-yourself activities elaborated and undertaken in the here and now. We first portray this anti-authoritarian community and outline debates around certain notions such as political action, power, and autonomy. The chapter then maps the variety of political actors and practices that shape the path towards the long-term goal of achieving collective autonomy.

Data and Methodology

The empirical analysis and argument presented in this paper draw from a collective research project conducted between 2005 and 2012 with the Research Group on Collective Autonomy (Collectif de recherche sur l'autonomie collective or CRAC), affiliated with Concordia University, in Montreal, Canada. The CRAC aimed to document and analyze contemporary initiatives of the anti-authoritarian movement that emerged in Quebec at the turn of this century. Being an anti-authoritarian profeminist research team, it used a prefigurative participatory action research methodology that integrated participants in all aspects of the research. CRAC members concretely experienced the antiauthoritarian perspective as their basis of affinity and had privileged contacts with the groups and networks involved in the research, accessing information essential to understanding the dynamics of anti-authoritarian movements.

The CRAC conducted 125 interviews with activists involved in nine different groups and networks of the anti-authoritarian community.[2] The persons interviewed represented a variety of activists involved in these groups and networks for different periods of time between 2000 and 2010. The interviews were also supported by the analysis of primary sources produced by these groups and networks (press releases, manifestos, declarations, websites, journals, etc.). These data were then used to produce case studies of individual groups and networks published in the form of monographs (CRAC 2008a; CRAC 2008b; CRAC 2010a; CRAC 2010b) or book chapters (Breton 2013; Eslami and Maynard 2013; Leblanc 2013) and served as the basis for transversal analysis on specific themes (CRAC 2011a; 2011b; 2011c; Breton et al. 2012a; 2012b, Sarrasin et al. 2012; Jeppesen et al. 2014).

An Anti-Authoritarian Community in Quebec

Although traces of anti-authoritarianism in social struggles in Quebec can be located as far back as the end of the eighteenth century (Dupuis-Déri 2008; Houle-Courcelles 2008), ideas and practices associated with this perspective resurfaced at the turn of the twenty-first century amidst the Global Justice cycle of protest (Lamoureux 2008; Hammond-Callaghan and Hayday 2008). This cycle of protest allowed for a renewed expression of this perspective in the province through the consolidation of an anti-authoritarian social movement community. In Quebec, the impulse for the public emergence of this community was given by the popular mobilization around the Summit of the Americas conference held in Quebec City in 2001 to discuss the proposed Free Trade Agreement of the Americas (FTAA) (Gaudet and Sarrasin 2008). In spite of a lower-intensity contention period that followed the 2001 mobilization against the FTAA, the contemporary anti-authoritarian perspective was carried on to the present day by diverse activist groups and networks organizing on various issues of struggle. The term anti-authoritarian is used by many activists of this community to designate their political work, some of them explicitly stating an anarchist allegiance, while others refusing all forms of ideological labels.

The anti-authoritarian groups and networks active in Quebec address several disparate but inter-connected issues of struggle. Together, they form a social movement community (Sarrasin et al. 2012), that is a loose grouping of spaces, networks and collectives united by a shared political culture and organizational interface (Buechler 1990; Staggenborg 1998; 2013; Taylor and Whittier 1992; Bereni and Revillard 2012). Activists rely on a variety of organizational forms within the collectivity, some of them more formally structured than others, on the basis of affinities articulated around a specific area of struggle (CRAC 2011a). The community can be subdivided into issue-related groupings formed out of diverse combinations of non-mixed collectives, affinity groups, and informal networks of collaborating activists, with many struggles occurring at the overlap of two or more issues (CRAC 2011: 3).[3]

Examples of groupings from the anti-authoritarian community include activists addressing radical ecology and organizing on issues such as environmental justice and food security.[4] Another one formed around radical feminism and profeminism, with activists fighting patriarchy and sexism.[5]

Organizing around radical queer politics, a third grouping involves activists working on queer, trans, anti-heteronormative, and anti-homonormative issues.[6] Anti-racism, anti-colonialism, and anti-imperialism are the issues forming the basis of affinity of another grouping organizing on issues related to (im)migrant and refugee rights or international solidarity.[7] Last but not least, an anti-capitalist and anti-state grouping involves activists fighting police brutality, workers' rights, poverty, gentrification, and prisons.[8]

Activists involved in this anti-authoritarian community share common features, such as:

1. The refusal of all systems of authority deemed illegitimate (capitalism, patriarchy, imperialism, colonialism, racism, ableism, etc.) and the promotion of alternative values such as social justice, mutual aid, solidarity, freedom, equality, spontaneity, autonomy, democracy, respect for diversity, and creativity (CRAC 2011: 5);

2. The use of direct action and the respect for a diversity of tactics;

3. Organizational forms based on direct democracy and the decentralization of power (CRAC 2011a, Sarrasin et al 2012).

These common characteristics form a political culture that is enacted in the practices developed by activists and put forward in a dual strategy of confrontation, aiming to destabilize the current socio-political order, and of construction, building grassroots alternatives (Jeppesen et al. 2014: 7). According to this strategy, anti-authoritarian activists aim to challenge capitalism and other systems of oppression by organizing campaigns which disrupt the established order. At the same time, they also engage on a day-to-day basis in the practice of prefiguration, a politics of the act that embodies concrete alternatives to the state and the market's model of social relations.[9] Social and political change thus unveils through this dual, long-term process of confrontation with authorities and construction of an organizational infrastructure for the anti-authoritarian community. It embodies the anti-authoritarian political ideal of a society built on the project of collective autonomy.

Collective Autonomy as a Political Project

Whereas, following its etymological meaning, the term "autonomy" refers to the idea of regulation by the self, to qualify it as collective refers to an enlarged meaning encompassing a social context for the construction and exercise of autonomy (Katsiaficas 2001: 548). Moreover, understanding collective autonomy as a political project implies revisiting conventional conceptions of political action and power as enacted by social movements and, by extension, of the phenomena considered to be part of the political sphere more generally.

The Political Action of Social Movements

A preliminary understanding of a social movements' political action locates the latter in the dimensions of its interventions that lie outside the immediate interests of its members (Boudreau 2015: 50). In this sense, political action unfolds when a movement engages in social debates that lie outside of its habitual sphere of action. In Quebec, this interpretation of the political action of social movements is often applied to the analysis of the workers' movement and to trade unions' action when these actors outgrow the strict defense of their members' interests and choose to intervene in the public sphere on issues touching upon the definition of the public good. This was the case in the fall of 2015 in the province of Quebec, when workers from the public sector and their trade unions, while negotiating their new collective agreement, engaged in wider debates on the accessibility of public services and the impact of austerity measures put forward by the government led by the Liberal Party of Quebec. This understanding of the political action of social movements thus connects their political dimension with their interactions with the polity, through their relations with state institutions, their participation in consultative processes, their members' social responsibility as active citizens, and their strategies to influence power holders or eventually take control of governmental power through a more formal vehicle such as a political party.

Such a conception of the political dimension of social movements as it relates to state institutions echoes the political process approach in social movement studies. This approach allows for analyses of social movements that take into consideration the structural environment in which movements develop. It distinguishes members of the polity who participate in institutional politics and have regular access to the resources of the state—i.e., the *insiders*—from actors located outside of this sphere who only aim to access it—i.e., the *outsiders* (Tilly 1978; McAdam 1982; Tarrow 1998; McAdam et al. 2001).

While this approach is useful to understand the external conditions that impact the emergence or decline of a social movement in each institutional context, it perpetuates a limited understanding of the political action of movements as it neglects what is happening beyond their interaction with the state. It also emphasizes an event-related view of social movements as they appear to the surface when mobilized in protest events but tend to fade away in periods of lower-intensity contention (Goodwin et Jasper 1999; Mathieu 2002; Snow 2004; Staggenborg et Taylor 2005; Armstrong et Bernstein 2008; Ancelovici et Rousseau 2009; Dufour et Goyer 2009).

Understanding the political dimensions of social movements as they relate to the state is akin to a dominant conception of politics in the field of political science. As state institutions have become the dominant form of political organization in contemporary societies, and since representative democracy is the main mechanism allowing for the embodiment of these institutions, legitimate forms of power are often associated with elected governments and certain processes that lead to the conquest of state power. Such processes often exclude groups that are marginalized by the ruling class (Fraser 2001).

A more comprehensive understanding of politics can be constructed on the conception of power as the capacity of individuals and groups to make decisions collectively, as it relates to the governance of their collectivity. In this view, power remains relational as it is located in the space that links individuals to one another but does not necessarily involve an individual or group's political domination over others (Arendt 2001; Castoriadis 2010). In this sense, power refers to the capacity of individuals to act together. It leads to the recognition of political phenomena occurring outside the relation to state institutions, in initiatives where a plurality of voices is expressed to forge a conception of the public good and where decisions are made by the collective (Rancière 1998).

Defining and Deconstructing Collective Autonomy

At the core of the collective autonomy project of the anti-authoritarian community lies the principle of self-determination, the idea that people involved in a particular situation are best located to collectively determine their needs and how they wish to function (CRAC 2011b). In addition to self-determination, collective autonomy is anchored in the principle of self-organization, the idea that self-determined collectives will also develop the means to organize themselves and carry out the decisions collectively negotiated. Through the principles of self-determination and self-organization, collective autonomy aims for the construction of a commons as an alternative to the state and the market: a "social systems in which resources are shared by a community of users/producers, who also define the modes of use and production, distribution, and circulation of these resources through democratic and horizontal forms of governance" (De Angelis and Harvie 2014: 280, cited in Jeppesen et al. 2014).

From the standpoint of the anti-authoritarian community, the choice in favor of collective autonomy is coherent with a political discourse that is critical of the way state institutions reproduce inequalities. Autonomous politics thus thrive "outside the power of the state and its mechanisms of representation as a constituent power, a free association of constitutive social forces" (McDonald 2007: 56). Activists in the community aim to develop independent of the state, but also separate from political parties and trade unions, as they can be vehicles of political intervention. Moreover, they tend to adopt corollary stances against other forms of systemic oppression such as capitalism and patriarchy, experimenting with practices that aim to emancipate people from the dominant structures that reproduce hierarchies. In other words,

> The goal of autonomous social movements is the subversion of politics: the decolonization of everyday life and civil society, not the conquest of state power. Based on a politics of the first person and a desire to create direct democracy, these movements oppose the false universality of the control

center under whose guise behemoth governments and corporations seek to impose their wills. (Katsiaficas 2001: 555)

Therefore, the political project of the anti-authoritarian community ultimately aims to change the form of dominant structures, not simply influence their content (Day 2005: 88). Nevertheless, to be fully grasped, collective autonomy also needs to be analyzed in a way that acknowledges how unequal power relations are dealt with in day-to-day modes of resistance by the community, on the basis of concrete social experiences that attempt to build alternatives to dominant structures. Approaching collective autonomy as a process thus involves complicating our understanding of autonomous practices to highlight the various ways in which they unfold to create a repertoire of diverse forms of resistance.

A first way to explore collective autonomy as a process is to identify the various spheres in which it is undertaken by activists. For example, practices of autonomy can be enacted in the political, economic, social, or cultural spheres of social movements (on this matter, also see Anna Kruzynski's chapter in this book). Since these spheres are interconnected, autonomous practices might progress simultaneously in the various spheres, but activists may also choose to focus on one aspect more than others and collective autonomy may progress at different rhythms in each of the spheres.

For example, an initiative such as a workers' cooperative may have developed practices of economic self-determination but still lack autonomous practices dealing with the reproduction of gendered or racialized social relations. Furthermore, even when concentrating on one specific sphere of action, deconstructing the various dimensions of autonomous practices within that sphere is an additional way of approaching autonomous practices as a process.

Looking at collective autonomy as a political process allows us to recognize how practices based on self-determination and self-organization may develop in differentiated ways for actors of the anti-authoritarian community. In this perspective, collective autonomy is a process built through time and at diverse rhythms according to the various spheres in which it unfolds. Although ultimately aiming at the dismantlement of dominant institutions, collective autonomy as a process does not imply that independence from external institutions will be immediately achieved, but rather, it involves progressively working towards self-determination and self-organization.

A Diversity of Anti-Authoritarian Political Practices

Based on accounts of contemporary anti-authoritarian organizing in Quebec as documented by the CRAC, the section that follows proposes an exploratory deconstruction of the various practices that form collective autonomy as a process and that have been undertaken by diverse actors within the community. Collective autonomy is portrayed as occurring through a diversity of internal political practices (i.e., intra-group relations), as well as external political practices (i.e., relations with other actors).

Internal Political Practices of Organizing

Collective autonomy is enacted in the anti-authoritarian community through an organizing structure that allows activists to act on the basis of shared affinities and needs. As mentioned earlier, the community is made up of overlapping groups and collectives organizing around different thematic issues. Activists in these groups and collectives come together around affinities based on identities, interests, or localities. The Centre social autogéré (Self-Managed Social Centre) in the Pointe-Saint-Charles neighborhood of Montreal is an example of people living in the same geographical area organizing against gentrification.[10] Another example of affinity-based organizing enacting internal political practices of collective autonomy is Montreal's Ste-Emilie Skillshare Collective, in which people self-identify as an intentional family based on a shared queer, trans, and BIPOC identity.

Affinity groups and collectives working on interconnected issues maintain sustained links to one another through a dynamic of networking. The networking structure in the anti-authoritarian community is flexible and decentralized, allowing for self-determination and self-organization to be enacted by activists who coalesce in action campaigns according to their needs. As an example, anti-racist/anti-colonial/anti-imperialist and radical queer networks regularly work on campaigns together around migration issues and the Israeli occupation of

Palestinian territories. Also, temporary coalitions are created when activists come together in campaigns of disruption against governmental summits or for mobilization on annual events, such as the International Women's Day on March 8th.

Aside from these public moments of mobilization, internal political practices of organizing also occur in the day-to-day practices of the anti-authoritarian community through the creation of counter-institutions and shared resources that form an organizational interface (Adamovsky 2008). This infrastructure is made up of autonomous community spaces, products, and services where prefigurative practices are constructed by activists as alternatives to the resources typically provided by the state or the market. For example, training can be offered through popular education workshops, like the ones put on at the annual community get-together of the Montreal Anarchist Bookfair.[11] Goods like vegetables and fruits are produced and distributed by autonomous garden initiatives, and do-it-yourself practices are taught at some of the bike repair skillshare workshops offered by members of the community.

The intention underlying these counter-institutions and resources is to allow people to self-organize on the basis of collectively-determined needs and effectively undermine the logic of the dominant system. In building these prefigurative practices, anti-authoritarians aim to put into action norms that encourage the development equality and cooperation opposing dominant norms of social relations based on individualism and competition. In this sense, within these spaces, they state their refusal of any behaviors that exhibit forms of oppression (like sexism, racism, heterosexism, colonialism, or ableism, for example). Instead, they emphasize respect for others when speaking and listening and are intolerant of oppressive communication. As expressed by an activist from the Montreal queer collective Les Panthères roses (The Pink Panthers):

> I don't believe in the complete change of the world tomorrow morning, but for me it's already very important to be able to create spaces where political ideas can really be put into practices, my political ideas must be put into practice. That I am able to live according to my ideas, I think it is already an enormous job. It is really very difficult. Anyway, for me, it allows me to go out into the world outside, which

is savage, and to be able to survive because I feel well. (cited in Jeppesen 2014: 887)

Nevertheless, anti-authoritarian activists reflect on the impact of their internal practices and consider how it effects the designing of collective autonomy. They understand the limitations involved in this approach. As such, avoiding a possible reproduction of the service provision approach offered by some of the more conventional nonprofit organizations (NGOs) of which anti-authoritarians are critical and moving away from, autonomist groups seek to further the outreach of anti-authoritarian political culture. According to some anti-authoritarian activists, this might involve strategically rethinking the "autonomous from the state and capitalism" stance of collective autonomy in order to not "just be *autonomous from*, but *compete with* dominant institutions" as a movement-building orientation that reinvents the idea of "serving the people" (Dixon 2014, 139).

Internal Political Practices of Deliberation and Decision-Making

Direct or radical democracy lies at the heart of collective autonomy practices undertaken by activists from the anti-authoritarian community. Whether it is in affinity group meetings or networking assemblies, they put forward practices of deliberation and decision making that rest on the objective of creating spaces of potentiality where a plurality of voices and experiences can be expressed (Roy-Allard 2016). This is achieved through a variety of practices collectively established so as to substitute hierarchical modes of organization like the ones implied in representative democracy. They strive to promote equality in the participation of individuals and the development of emancipatory social relations.

Practices of deliberation and decision-making not only favor the power to act by allowing individual expression, but also by encouraging activists to take into account their particular social positions in relation to others. These practices contribute to the becoming of individual political subjects, as activists expand their understanding of power relations and of their own social positions in the dynamics of oppression (Rancière 1998). It also allows the community to become a collective political subject, as the anti-authoritarian identity is constantly being defined and reaffirmed through this process of deliberation and decision-making.

This conception of democracy as a site of individual and collective empowerment and becoming is put into practice through mechanisms favoring decentralization and horizontalism (Maeckelbergh 2011). For one thing, consensus-based decision making is favored, allowing individuals who disagree with a given proposal to express their dissent and contribute to the collective remodeling of the proposal. Other practices encouraging the expression of a diversity of opinions include alternating speaking lists between women and men or giving priority to first interventions. Emotional dynamics that may potentially lead to power issues are also addressed through practices that emphasize effective dimensions and care, such as check-ins and check-outs at the beginning and end of meetings allowing people to share personal experiences and discuss how they feel about the meeting or the designation of a vibe-minder to track the emotional tenor of the meeting (Jeppesen et al. 2014).

Non-mixed caucuses allow for people who feel the need to deliberate about an issue in the context of their specific identity—such as women, people of colour, or queer people—to deliberate in spaces where they feel more secure and freer to raise certain issues. Decentralization is ensured by encouraging the rotation of tasks, like facilitation of an assembly. As people engage in these practices, "they develop alternative capacities by creating relationships that replace socio-cultural norms of domination with cooperation, active listening, collective self-care and consensus building" (Jeppesen et al. 2014, 888).

Again, this process is not without challenges. Although they are critical of a top-down model of leadership shaped by patriarchal stereotypes and other modes of social domination (Dixon 2014), anti-authoritarian practices of deliberation and decision-making are not exercised in the total absence of leadership. Capacities based on skills, knowledge, practical experiences, or personal aptitudes do affect activists' capabilities to engage in practices of deliberation and decision-making. Overcoming this reality in the aim of achieving horizontal and egalitarian relationships implies acknowledging these differences and determining mechanisms that will allow for collective benefits.

External Political Practices of Interaction with Social Actors

Considering collective autonomy as a process unveils the diversity of tactics that make up the anti-authoritarian community's approach to political transformation. Although the disruption of dominant institutions remains an important goal for anti-authoritarian activists, seizing state power is not the objective of their organizing. Rather, change is considered to occur gradually, mainly by experimenting horizontal social relations in the construction of alternatives. Prefigurative practices disseminating the anti-authoritarian political culture are thus not only shared within spaces of the community but also outwards with other social actors through a non-hierarchical process of "cross-pollination" as interactions occur (CRAC 2011b; Jeppesen et al. 2014).

Among its particularities, Quebec's social scene is composed of a dynamic patchwork of collective actors, from less formally structured social movements like the anti-authoritarian community to a vast network of more institutionalized community organizations (Dufour 2007). This context that emerges from past and present popular mobilizations is marked by a certain proximity between these actors, through relationships oscillating between collaboration and opposition.

Many community organizations, for example, are integrated into the province's governance structure and depend on it for funding, while at the same time, try to maintain a critical stance towards the state and capitalism. The anti-authoritarian community that has emerged in this context at the turn of the twenty-first century maintains close ties with the community organization network, through punctual joint campaigns or the fact that some anti-authoritarian activists occupy professional positions in these organizations (Phebus 2013). Therefore, formal and informal interactions with social actors outside of the community occur as mobilizations are jointly developed or as day-to-day contacts happen, allowing for the dissemination of the anti-authoritarian political culture of self-determination and self-organization.

The respect for a diversity of tactics according to situations and needs is an important aspect of this political culture. Anti-authoritarian activists regularly engage in struggles with individuals directly affected by a given situation and according to the needs they express, for example, on migrant issues where people face deportation. Such practice involves being in solidarity with those on the front-line of an issue, adopting a position of ally (CRAC 2011c). This community-based work takes place when people most affected are speaking and acting for themselves, determining orientations and taking leadership roles, but are not necessarily at the forefront of the protest, like facing down police lines or undertaking complicated administrative paperwork. Anti-authoritarians will thus choose to organize where people are located and use their own social locations, sometimes being one of privilege, in order to support these struggles. Julie, an activist in the anti-colonial and anti-racism network in Montreal, expressed it this way:

> It's important to send a message of solidarity, to send a message to the people that are directly affected "you're not alone, and other people care." I think it's important to send a message to the oppressors that there's no universal consent to the oppression. For example, a message being sent to the Canadian government...that not all people in Canada think that's it okay that Canada is being complicit in the bombing of Gaza. And also, it's an important way of using that privilege. Sometimes you just have more access to power structures, or more leeway to take certain risks. (cited in Jeppesen et al. 2014: 889)

This community-based work sometimes implies working closely with mainstream community organizations and local institutions that might not share the anti-authoritarian political culture. However, as they get involved with these actors in front-line struggles, activists put their vision into practice by supporting spaces where people can come together around concrete experiences of self-determination and self-organization. For example, activists will encourage community support with and for migrant people and their family. For anti-authoritarian activists, engaging in a strategy of immediate struggles with diverse social actors is thus a way to recognize the lived realities of oppression, without necessarily trading off the whole process of collective autonomy.

External Political Practices of Interaction with Political Actors

In the same vein, engaging in front-line struggles means in some cases demanding an intervention by the very state anti-authoritarian activists want to abolish. For actors in the anti-authoritarian community, this is coherent with the fact that collective autonomy practices account for modes of crisis intervention when survival is at stake, as mentioned by an activist from Montreal's radical feminist network:

> I have no qualms about taking a woman to a women's shelter, even if that women's shelter doesn't accept trans women or women who don't have immigration papers. If the woman that I'm working with is going to be not killed by her spouse if I take her to that women's shelter, and *is* going to be killed by her spouse if I don't, I'm going to take her. (cited in Jeppesen 2014: 891)

The strategic engagement with front-line struggles implies that reforms can be advocated for, and state-designed social programs can be defended if they concretely improve people's lives, even if these reforms do not lead to large-scale transformation. For example, activists from the Montreal Solidarity Across Borders network are involved in the "Solidarity City" campaign so that undocumented (im)migrants and refugees have access to essential services such as health care, education, and other social services.[12] The campaign mainly calls upon local communities to practice tangible mutual aid and solidarity with undocumented migrants by not asking or revealing their status. It also rests on frequent interaction with governmental agencies like the Canadian Border Services Agency (CBSA) or the Centre de services scolaire (school board) of Montreal, as well as deputies, local counselors, and school counselors for preventing arrests, detention, and deportation of migrant individuals.

Again, such interactions with dominant political actors do not necessarily compromise the long term anti-authoritarian process of collective autonomy. They are rather seen as a short-term strategic maneuver in the pursuit of longer-term political goals. These instrumental types of collaboration in front-line struggles are considered legitimate by activists as long as there is no internal interference of institutionalized political actors into anti-authoritarian group dynamics regarding the definition of political orientations and strategic choices. Moreover, while adopting such a strategic stance with dominant political actors, anti-authoritarian activists still oppose the logic of hierarchical institutions by organizing according to their internal practices of collective autonomy. The focus remains on building individual and collective power among oppressed groups, by "bringing self-determination and self-organization in an issue usually guided by state logics" (Dixon 2014: 131).

Conclusion

Building upon an empirical portrait of the anti-authoritarian social movement community in Quebec as it has developed at the turn of this century, this chapter has illustrated the various political practices that make up the process of collective autonomy: namely intra-political practices of organizing, intra-political practices of deliberation and decision-making, extra-political practices of interaction with social actors, and extra-political practices of interaction with political actors. It was argued that deconstructing the process of collective autonomy into various spheres of action and, moreover, into various dimensions in each of those spheres, allows for a nuanced understanding of how collective autonomy actually unfolds, illustrating the complexity of power relations engaged in by actors in the anti-authoritarian community.

In a broader perspective, considering collective autonomy as a process unveils political action as also occurring outside of partisan politics. For analysts and activists of social movements, it supports the acknowledgment of collective autonomy as a political ideal even when interactions with dominant institutions occur, moving beyond a dichotomous conception of autonomous politics as being either "in or against" those institutions.

The repertoire of practices that make up for the process of collective autonomy shows instead that anti-authoritarian activists deal with certain tensions as they work towards their long-term political goal. They build concrete prefigurative alternatives based on self-determination and self-organization, while also sometimes dealing with the state and other mainstream actors in struggles against the realities of social domination. It demonstrates that a space of contiguity with external actors and conventional politics exists in collective autonomy and affects the dynamics of autonomous movements, provided activists engage consciously in the endorsement of these interactions. Approaching collective autonomy as a process designed by a diversity of actors and practices thus allows us to expand our understanding of the political dimension of these initiatives, and of how anti-authoritarian activists manage to "be in the world, but not of it" (Dixon 2014: 125).

Endnotes

1 Authors have used different terms to describe these forms of resistance, such as autonomous politics, anti-authoritarian movements or horizontalism, but it is arguable that they all share common attributes such as decision-making processes and organizational mechanisms aiming for the dismantlement of domination and the development of egalitarian social relations.

2 The groups and networks involved in CRAC's study are Ainsi squattent-elles, Liberterre, Les Panthères roses, Qteam, Ste-Emilie Skillshare, the Autonmous Gardens, the radical feminist network, the anti-colonial and anti-racism network and the Convergence des luttes anticapitalistes (CLAC).

3 CRAC members have argued elsewhere that some of these groupings form micro-cohorts within the anti-authoritarian movement (Breton et al. 2012a; 2012b). Following Nancy Whittier's proposal (1997), micro-cohorts are conceived as "clusters of participants who enter a social movement within a year or two of each other and are shaped by distinct transformative experiences that differ because of subtle shifts in the political context" (1997: 762).

4 Groups and networks from that grouping involved in CRAC's study included The Liberterre Collective (CRAC 2008a), an eco-anarchist group that existed in Montreal mainly between 2003 and 2006, as well as two autonomous garden experiences from the greater Montreal area (CRAC 2010b). Other collectives from that grouping include the People's Potato and Midnight Kitchen, two collectively run food groups dedicated to providing affordable and healthy food.

5 The CRAC worked with activists from the radical feminist network involved in various autonomous groups and collectives over the years, such as "les Sorcières, Némésis, les Amères Noélles, les Insoumises, les Amazones, Rebelles sans frontières, Les femmes ont faim, Cyprine, les Féministes radicales de l'UQAM, les Fallopes, Groupe FEMMES sororitaires, les Lilithantes and La riposte" (Breton et al. 2012a, 150), as well as the Ainsi squattent-elles collective, a radical feminist collective based in Quebec City (CRAC 2008b). Page (2006), Blais (2008) and Leblanc (2013) offer an overview of contemporary radical feminism in Montreal, the latter as part of CRAC's research project.

6 Radical queer politics is an expression designating a particular analysis of

queer issues as necessarily related to the fight against capitalism and state power, as distinct from more mainstream currents of queer politics which seek recognition from state or capitalist institutions. Les Panthères roses was among the first radical queer collectives to appear in Montreal's activist scene and existed as a group from 2002 to 2007, dedicated to the fight against pink capitalism, heteronormative society, and binary gender rules (CRAC 2010a.) QTeam is a Montreal-based, radical queer collective which formed in 2007 out of an initiative by members of the former Anti-Capitalist Ass Pirates collective. No longer active as a collective, many of QTeam's members are still involved in organizing radical queer events. Ste-Emilie Skillshare is an autonomous community art space based in Montreal.

7 This grouping is composed of activists from groups such as No One is Illegal, struggling collectively for the self-determination of migrants and indigenous peoples, or Solidarity Across Borders, a migrant justice network based in Montreal.

8 The Convergence des luttes anticapitalistes (CLAC) first formed in 2001 to oppose the Summit of the Americas in Quebec City (Gaudet and Sarrasin 2008; Breton 2013). The development of the Centre social autogéré (Autonomous Social Centre) is an ongoing project in the Pointe-Saint-Charles neighbourhood of Montreal, an initiative of which Anna Kruzynski dresses an account in another chapter of this book. The Collectif opposé à la brutalité policière (Collective Opposed to Police Brutality) is an autonomous group active since 1995.

9 Prefiguration is a term used to refer to one's desire to make means and ends mutually constitutive in a struggle (Breines 1989; Polletta 2002; Milstein 2010; Maeckelbergh 2011; Ancelovici 2016).

10 See Anna Kruzynski's chapter in this book for more details on the project.

11 The Montreal Anarchist Bookfair (Salon du livre anarchiste de Montréal) is an annual event that brings together individuals from North America and beyond, sharing their publications and materials on anarchist and anti-authoritarian organizing. Activities and workshops are also organized during the event. It has played an important role in the building of the anti-authoritarian community in Quebec since 2000.

12 For more information on the campaign, see http://www.solidarityacrossborders.org/en/solidarity-city.

References

Adamovsky, Ezequiel. 2008. "Autonomous Politics and Its Problems: Thinking the Passage from Social to Political." In Chris Spannos (ed.) *Real Utopia: Participatory Society for the 21st Century*. Oakland : AK Press, 346-362.

Ancelovici, Marcos and Stéphanie Rousseau. 2009. "Présentation. Les mouvements sociaux et la complexité institutionnelle." *Sociologie et sociétés* 41 (2) : 5-14

Ancelovici, Marcos. 2016. "Occupy Montreal and the Politics of Horizontalism." In Marcos Ancelovici, Pascale Dufour and Heloise Nez (eds.), *Street Politics in the Age of Austerity: From the Indignados to Occupy*, Amsterdam: Amsterdam University Press,

Arendt, Hannah. 2001. *Qu'est-ce que la politique ?*. Paris: Seuil.

Armstrong, Elizabeth et Mary Bernstein. 2008. "Culture, Power and Institutions: A Multi Institutional Politics Approach to Social Movements." *Sociological Theory* 26 (1): 74-99.

Beaupré- Laforest, Catherine. 2008. « Québec solidaire, analyse et défis de la gauche électorale québécoise contemporaine ». In Francis Dupuis-Déri (ed.), *Québec en mouvements. Idées et pratiques militantes contemporaines*. Montréal : Lux éditeur, 131-146.

Bereni, Laure and Anne Révillard. 2012. « Un mouvement social paradigmatique? Ce que le mouvement des femmes fait à la sociologie des mouvements sociaux ». *Sociétés contemporaines* 85: 17-41.

Bey, Hakim. 1991. *TAZ. The Temporary Autonomous Zone, Ontological Anarchy, Poetic Terrorism*. New York: Autonomedia.

Blais, Melissa. 2008. « Féministes radicales et hommes proféministes : l'alliance piégée ». In Francis Dupuis-Déri (ed.), *Québec en mouvements. Idées et pratiques militantes contemporaines*. Montréal: Lux éditeur, 147-176.

Boudreau, Philippe. 2015. *La politisation comme composante active de l'évolution de la culture mouvementiste: étude du rapport à l'action politique de trois mouvements sociaux québécois, 1980-2009*. Doctoral dissertation. Ottawa: University of Ottawa.

Breines, Wini. 1989. *Community and Organization in the New Left, 1962-1968: The Great Refusal*. Rutgers University Press.

Breton, Émilie. 2013. « La CLAC : portrait d'un réseau anticapitaliste ». In Rémi Bellemare-Caron, Émilie Breton, Marc-André Cyr, Francis Dupui-Déri and Anna Kruzynski (eds), *Nous sommes ingouvernables. Les anarchistes au Québec aujourd'hui*. Montréal: Lux éditeur : 41-62.

Breton, Émilie, Sandra Jeppesen, Anna Kruzynski and Rachel Sarrasin. 2012a. "Feminisms at the heart of contemporary anarchism in Québec: Grassroots practices of intersectionality." *Canadian Woman Studies* 29 (3): 147-159.

_____. 2012b. "Prefigurative Self-governance and Self-organization: the Influence of Antiauthoritarian (Pro)feminist, Radical Queer and Antiracist Networks in Quebec." In Aziz Choudry, Jill Hanley and Eric Shragge (eds), *Organize!: Building from the Local for Global Justice*. Oakland: PM Press, 156-173.

Buechler, Steven M.1990. *Women's Movements in the United States*. New Brunswick, New Jersey: Rutgers University Press.

Castells, Manuel. 2005. «Neoanarquismo». *Diario de la Vanguardia de Barcelona* (Barcelona), 21 mai.

Castoriadis, Cornelius. 2010. *Démocratie et relativisme.* Paris : Milles et une nuits.

Collectif de recherche sur l'autonomie collective. 2008a. *Collectif Liberterre. Une monographie.* Montréal : CRAC.

————. 2008b. *Ainsi squattent-elles! Une monographie.* Montréal : CRAC. En ligne : http://www.crac-kebec.org/node/90

————. 2010a. *Les Panthères Roses de Montréal : Un collectif queer d'actions directes.* Montréal : CRAC. En ligne : http://www.crac-kebec.org/bibliotheque/les-pantheres-roses-de-montreal-une-monographie.

————. 2010b. *Une révolution peut commencer par un seul brin de paille. Portrait de deux jardins autogérés de la grande région de Montréal.* Montréal : CRAC. En ligne : http://www.crac-kebec.org/bibliotheque/monographie-une-revolution-peut-commencer-par-un-seul-brin-de-paille

————. 2011a. *Antiautoritaires au Québec : uni.es par une culture poli'tique.*Working paper. http://www.crac-kebec.org/files/1-cracculture_politiquev2_19oct2011_en.pdf

————. 2011b. *Vision du changement social : l'anarchisme en tant que processus.* Working paper. http://www.crac-kebec.org/files/2-cracanar_processusv2_19oct2011_en.pdf.

————. 2011. *Intersectionnalité, anti-oppression et 'front lines struggles'.* Working paper http://www.crac-kebec.org/files/workshop_anti-opp_vs_may_2011.pdf.

Day, Richard. 2005. *Gramsci is Dead. Anarchist Currents in the Newest Social Movements.* London/New York: Pluto Press.

————. 2004. "From Hegemony to Affinity: The Political Logic of the Newest Social Movements." *Cultural Studies* 18: 716-748.

Dinerstein, Ana C. 2015. *The Politics of Autonomy in Latin America. The Art of Organising Hope.* London : Palgrave Macmillan.

Dixon, Chris. 2014. *Another Politics. Talking Across Today's Transformative Movements.* Oakland : University of California Press.

Dufour, Pascale. 2007. « La politisation du milieu communautaire au Québec ». In Jane Jenson, Berengère Marques-Pereira and Éric Remacle. *L'état des citoyennetés en Europe et dans les Amériques.* Montréal : Presses de l'Université de Montréal, 243-265.

Dufour, Pascale and Renaud Goyer. 2009. « Analyse de la transnationalisation de l'action collective. Proposition pour une géographie des solidarités transnationales ». *Sociologie et sociétés* 41 (2) : 111-134.

Dupuis-Déri, Francis. 2008. « Pistes pour une histoire de l'anarchisme au Québec ». *Bulletin d'histoire politique* 16 (2): 287-302.

Epstein, Barbara. 2001. "Anarchism and the Anti-Globalization Movement." *Monthly Review* 53 (4).

Eslami Shirene and Robyn Maynard. 2013. « L'antiracisme et l'anticolonial-isme au cœur des luttes antiautoritaires ». In Rémi Bellemare-Caron, Émilie Breton, Marc-André Cyr, Francis Dupuis-Déri and Anna Kruzynski (eds), *Nous sommes ingouvernables. Les anarchistes au Québec aujourd'hui*. Montréal : Lux éditeur, 203-224.

Fraser, Nancy. 2001. « Repenser la sphère publique: une contribution à la critique de la démocratie telle qu'elle existe vraiment », *Hermès* 31 : 125-156.

Flesher Fominaya, Cristina. 2007. "Autonomous Movements and the Institutional Left: Two Approaches in Tension in the Madrid's Anti-Globalization Network." *South European Society and Politics* 12 (3): 335-358.

Gaudet, Louis-Frédéric and Rachel Sarrasin. 2008. « Fragments d'anarchisme au Québec (2000-2006) ». In Francis Dupuis-Déri (ed.), *Québec en mouvements*. Montréal: Lux éditeur, 177-198.

Gibson-Graham, J. K. 1996. *The End of Capitalism (As We Knew It): A Feminist Critique of Political Economy*. Minneapolis: University of Minnesota Press.

Gibson-Graham, J.K. 2006. *A Post-capitalist Politics*. Minneapolis: University of Minnesota Press.

Gibson-Graham, J.K., Jenny Cameron and Stephen Healy. 2013. *Take Back the Economy: An Ethical Guide for Transforming Communities*. Minneapolis: University of Minnesota Press

Glasius Marlies and Geofrey Pleyers. 2013. "The Global Moment of 2011: Democracy, Social Justice and Dignity", *Development and Change* 43 (3): 547-567.

Goodwin, Jeff et James Jasper. 1999. "Caught in a Winding, Snarling Vine: The Structural Bias of Political Process Theory." *Sociological Forum* 14 (1): 27-54.

Gordon, Uri. 2008. *Anarchy Alive! Anti-Authoritarian Politics From Practice to Theory*. London: Pluto Press.

Graeber, David. 2002. "The New Anarchists." *New Left Review* 13 (janvier-février): 61-73.

_____. 2006. *Pour une anthropologie anarchiste*. Montréal: Lux éditeur.

_____. 2013. *The Democracy Project: A History, a Crisis, a Movement*. New York: Spiegel & Grau.

Hammond-Callaghan, Marie and Matthew Hayday (eds). 2008. *Mobilizations, Protests and Engagements. Canadian Perspectives on Social Movements*. Halifax: Fernwood Publishing.

Houle-Courcelles, Mathieu. 2008. *Sur les traces de l'anarchisme au Québec (1860-1960)*. Montréal : Lux éditeur.

Ibáñez, Tomás. 2014. *Anarchisme en mouvement. Anarchisme, néoanarchisme et postanarchisme*. Paris : Nada éditions.

Jeppesen, Sandra, Anna Kruzynski, Rachel Sarrasin, and Emilie Breton. 2014. The Anarchist Commons, *Ephemera: Theory and Politics in Organisation* 14 (4): 879-900.

Katsiaficas, George. 1997, 2006. *The Subversion of Politics: European Autonomous Social Movements and the Decolonization of Everyday Life.* Oakland: AK Press.

_____. 2001. "The Necessity of Autonomy," *New Political Science,* 23 (4): 547-555.

Lamoureux, Diane. 2008. « Québec 2001 : Un tournant pour les mouvements sociaux québécois? ». In Francis Dupuis-Déri (ed.), *Québec en mouvements. Idées et pratiques militantes contemporaines.* Montréal: Lux éditeur, 11-34.

Leblanc, Jacinthe. 2013. « Contre le patriarcat, je résiste et je me bats ». In Rémi Bellemare-Caron, Émilie Breton, Marc-André Cyr, Francis Dupuis-Déri and Anna Kruzynski (eds), *Nous sommes ingouvernables. Les anarchistes au Québec aujourd'hui.* Montréal : Lux éditeur, 241-254.

Luck, Simon. 2008. *Sociologie de l'engagement libertaire dans la France contemporaine.* Thèse de doctorat. Département de science politique. Université Paris 1 Panthéon-Sorbonne.

Maeckelbergh Marianne. 2011. "Doing is Believing: Prefiguration as Strategic Practice in the Alterglobalization Movement", *Social Movement Studies,* 10 (1): 1-20.

Mathieu, Lillian. 2002. « Rapport au politique, dimensions cognitives et perspectives pragmatiques dans l'analyse des mouvements sociaux ». *Revue française de science politique* 52 (1): 75-100.

McAdam, Doug. 1982. *Political Process and the Development of Black Insurgency, 1930-1970.* Chicago: University of Chicago Press.

McAdam, Doug, Sidney Tarrow and Charles Tilly. 2001. *Dynamics of Conten' tion.* Cambridge: Cambridge University Press.

Milstein, Cindy. 2010. *Anarchism and its Aspirations.* Oakland: Institute for Anarchist Studies/AK Press.

McDonald, Kevin. 2007. "Between Autonomy and Vulnerability: the Space of Movement", *Recherches sociologiques et anthropologiques* 38 (1), 49-63.

Pagé, Geneviève. 2006. *Reinventing the Wheel or Fixing It? A Case Study of Radical Feminism in Contemporary Montreal.* Masters dissertation. Carleton : Carleton University.

Phébus, Nicolas. 2013. « Des libertaires dans le mouvement communautaire populaire ». In Rémi Bellemare-Caron, Émilie Breton, Marc-Andé Cyr, Francis Dupui-Déri and Anna Kruzynski (eds), *Nous sommes ingouvernables. Les anarchistes au Québec aujourd'hui.* Montréal: Lux éditeur, 153-168.

Polletta, Francesca. 2002. *Freedom is an Endless Meeting. Democracy in American Social Movements.* Chicago: The University of Chicago Press.

Rancière, Jacques. 1998. *Aux bords du politique.* Paris : La fabrique .

Roy-Allard, Maxime. 2016. *De la démocratie à Montréal : Les assemblées populaires autonomes de quartier (APAQ).* Masters dissertation. Montréal : Université du Québec à Montréal.

Sarrasin, Rachel, Anna Kruzynski, Sandra Jeppesen and Émilie Breton. 2012. « Radicaliser l'action collective : portrait de l'option libertaire au Québec ». *Lien social et politiques* 68 : 141-166.

Snow, David A. 2004. "Social Movements as Challenges to Authority: Resistance to an Emerging Conceptual Hegemony." *Research in Social Movements, Conflicts and Change* 25: 3-25.

Staggenborg, Suzanne and Verta Taylor. 2005. "Whatever Happened to the Women's Movement?" *Mobilization: An International Journal* 10 (1): 37-52.

Staggenborg, Suzanne. 2013. "Organization and Community in Social Movements." In Jacquelien Van Stekelenburg, Conny Roggeband et Bert Klandermans (eds), *Dynamics, Mechanisms and Processes. The Future of Social Movement Research*. Minneapolis : University of Minnesota Press, 125-145.

_____. 1998. "Social Movement Communities and Cycles of Protest: The Emergence and Maintenance of a Local Women's Movement." *Social Problems* 45 (2): 180-204.

Tarrow, Sidney. 1998. *Power in Movement: Social Movements and Contentious Politics*. Cambridge: Cambridge University Press.

Taylor, Verta and Nancy Whittier. 1992. "Collective Identity in Social Movement Communities: Lesbian Feminist Mobilization." In Aldon D. Morris and Carol McClurg Mueller (eds), *Frontiers in Social Movement Theory*, New Haven : Yale University Press: 104-129.

Tilly, Charles. 1978. *From Mobilization to Revolution*. New York: McGraw-Hill Companies.

Whittier, Nancy. 1997. "Political Generations, Micro-Cohorts and the Transformation of Social Movements." *American Sociological Review* 62 (5): 760-778.

Chapter 6

Collective Autonomy in Action:
From the Autonomous
Social Centre to Building 7

Anna Kruzynski
Concordia University, Canada

George Katsiaficas identifies two recent episodes of the international eros effect: the alterglobalization wave and anti-war protests at the end of the 1990s and early 2000s, and the Arab Spring and Occupy Movements of 2011 and beyond.[1] The eros effect, following Katsiaficas, "is crystalized in the sudden and synchronous international emergence of hundreds of thousands of people who occupy public space and call for a completely different political reality," based on "their common belief in new values," oftentimes in several places, at the same time (2011: 1). My work with the Research Group on Collective Autonomy (CRAC) demonstrated that that "collective unconscious" also erupted in the urban centers of Quebec (Sarrasin et al. 2016), manifesting in the anti-MAI, anti-FTAA, and anti-war revolts at the turn of the century (Dupuis-Déri 2008). In 2012, in the wake of Occupy (Ancelovici 2016), the city was the siege of massive student revolt (Ancelovici & Dupuis-Déri 2014). A general strike disrupted everyday life in most universities, colleges, and even some high schools. Daily (and nightly) snake marches, blockades of the port, and attacks on symbols of capitalist greed made headlines for months on end.

While not as widespread or historically anchored as in Europe, these moments of revolt share certain characteristics with the autonomous movements documented by Katsiaficas (2006). In Quebec, scholars of contention talk of the antiauthoritarian movement (Breton et al. 2015; Sarrasin et al. 2016) or contemporary anarchism (Bellemare-Caron et al. 2013; Jeppesen, Kruzynski et al. 2014). Affinity groups, collectives, and networks share a common political culture. They present (1) a political stance against exploitation and oppression in all its forms (including the state) and for respect, mutual aid and solidarity; (2) a two-pronged approach to social change that is operationalized, on the one hand, by confrontational and direct tactics to disrupt the status quo and, on the other, by the experimentation, in the here-and-now of subjectivities, relationships, and institutions coherent with the antiauthoritarian compass; and (3) a decentralized and non-hierarchical organizational form. The CRAC called this collective autonomy self-determination and self-organization; but in effect, we could have called it simply "autonomy" as does Katsiaficas, because the meaning is the same.

These movements are the training ground for many activists, myself included, who chose to channel our "hate...vis-à-vis external forces" (Katsiaficas 2001, citing Jung) and pour our "human solidarity and love of freedom" (Katsiaficas 2001, citing Marcuse) into the Autonomous Social Centre (ASC) of Pointe-Saint-Charles. Pointe-Saint-Charles, a post-industrial, traditionally working-class neighbourhood of Montreal, renowned as a bastion of strength, solidarity, and resistance, has managed to slow down the forces of gentrification in ways that adjacent neighbourhoods have not (Kruzynski 2020). Well-known, for example, is the successful campaign run by grassroots community organisations in 2006 to stop the plans of a capitalist developer to move the Montreal Casino to Pointe-Sainte Charles, along with a large-scale international conference center. In 2007, inspired by the Centri social in Rome, the Bookchin-inspired anarchist collective La Pointe libertaire put out a call to folks wanting to squat a vacant industrial building: "We want to open a space for collective autonomy to flower and for direct democracy to earn its reputation for excellence."[2] Hundreds responded to the call, and the ASC was born.

In this paper, using the example of the ASC, I will show how, at the local level, the activists transformed "public participation into something completely different from what is normally understood as political" (Katsiaficas 2006:6). I will discuss how they subvert politics, but also how they subvert economics and culture. To accomplish this, I will begin with a short chronological description of the story of the Autonomous Social Centre. Then, I will explore the political, cultural, and economic practices that were/are enacted by the ASC, bringing in different authors to feed the analysis. I will borrow from Katsiaficas and Marina Sitrin (2012; Sitrin & Azzelilini 2014), an engaged scholar of contemporary autonomous movements in Argentina, to flesh out political and cultural processes. For the economic processes, I will borrow from Julie Graham and Katherine Gibson, writing under the pseudonym of J.K. Gibson-Graham, who have developed a theory of economic self-determination based on over 30 years of empirical work in communities who are engaged in "taking back the economy" (1996, 2006). I will conclude by reflecting on revolution as process and on the necessity to document creative autonomy that already exists but is oftentimes hidden from view.

Before delving in however, a quick methodological note. The analysis herein is based on my personal experience within the ASC, on both internal and public documents produced by the ASC, and on the book written by my affinity group, La Pointe libertaire (2013), on the initial phases of the struggle. In addition, it is important to share that several of the activists at the core of the ASC participated in the research project conducted by CRAC. Given this, it is impossible to untangle my analysis from that of my comrades. I want to recognize their invaluable contribution to this work.[3]

My Story of the Autonomous Social Centre

Phase 1: The Squat

Following the public assembly that launched the ASC in 2007, hundreds of activists got involved in a two-year mobilization campaign that would lead to the squat of Seracon, an abandoned candle factory on the Lachine Canal. In order to gain support from our neighbours and local community organizations, many of whom were not convinced that squatting was a good way to counter gentrification,[4] we reclaimed public space, here and there, and did what we wanted to see emerge in our permanent space. Itinerant creative spontaneity (Katsiaficas 2006) by what we called "autonomous projects," actively "reclaiming the Point," mobilized hundreds of people who participated in bike repair workshops, open-air film screenings, dumpster-diving and food transformation, poetry readings, and concerts. On May 29, 2009, 500 people participated in the demonstration that enabled the opening of the squat, officially supported by 70 organizations across Quebec. Within 24 hours, we had set-up a kitchen, toilets, dormitories, and a stage. Just before the concert, the police force, snipers and all, evicted us *manu-militari*.

Phase 2: Peoples' Expropriation of Building 7

The sense of injustice and anger that was triggered by the eviction of Seracon was channeled, as of 2009, into a campaign to expropriate, for the collectivity, a 90,000 square foot industrial building on the CN rail yards, from capitalist developer Vincent Chiara (Mach Group). The ASC joined forces with grassroots community groups and more mainstream cultural organizations to form the *Collectif 7 à nous*.[5] After three years of struggle, we successfully pressured Chiara to donate Building 7 to us, decontaminated along with $1 million for renovations (La Pointe libertaire 2013; Kruzynski & Silvestro 2013; Triollet 2013). Unheard of in the recent history of Quebec, this peoples' victory was the result of a combination of factors. Most notable was the force of the outrage in the neighbourhood at the sale of the CN rail yards for $1 and the convergence of a diversity of actors who were able and willing to engage in a diversity of tactics (Silvestro 2012). While the well-connected and influential Darling Foundry engaged in direct negotiations with Chiara, the concerted-action round table Action-Watchdog, composed of 30 grass-roots community organizations kept on the heels of local politicians and organized symbolic actions to mobilize neighbourhood residents. The ASC, more confrontational, reclaimed Building 7 in the here-and-now, making it as though the Building was already ours. Without asking for permission, we squatted this private property for an afternoon, and then an evening.

Phase 3: Holding Down the Fort While Waiting for the Keys

From 2012 to 2017, the *Collectif 7 à nous*, now with legal status as a non-profit organization, valiantly held down the fort during the long and tedious negotiations involved in the transferring of the property. During this time, most activists involved in the ASC became disillusioned, bored, or simply fed up, and therefore pulled back. In 2013, in a general assembly, it was decided to put the ASC on standby until we had the keys to Building 7 in hand. A few anti-authoritarians from the inner circle remained involved in the *Collectif 7 à nous*, as board or committee members, or as paid staff. During this phase, architectural plans were drawn up, investments were sought out, a documentary film was made and cessation was negotiated.[6] The Building was officially transferred on April 28, 2017.

Phase 4: Manufacturing Collective Autonomy

It's winter 2017. Three million dollars has been scrounged up and renovations have begun! 150 people show up to a general assembly and the excitement is palpable. A *capharnaüm* of people from all walks of life, with tons of ideas, different experiences, who all want to be part of this historic moment: the "manufacturing of collective autonomy"[7] in a space of our own, Building 7. In the wake of this, the ASC emerges from hibernation, familiar faces long-time absent are back, as are new activists who got their feet wet for the first time in the wake of the student uprisings in 2012 and 2015. Three "autonomous" projects carried by anti-authoritarians are at the heart of the first stage of development of Building 7; the grocery store/café Le Detour; the brew-pub Les Sans-Tavernes; and the artistic foundry Coop La Coulée. Not to mention, on the one hand, the arcade and upcycling project by the youth-led cooperative Press Start, and, on the other, the 12,000 square feet of collaborative spaces (bike, auto, wood, ceramic, photo, printing, and silk-screening shops) and "the commons," a multi-function space with meeting rooms, a kitchen, showers, and storage.

Stage two is the services axis (childcare, birthing, family, and alternative health centers), stage three is the food production/transformation/distribution axis, and stage four is the contemporary art axis carried by the Darling Foundry (artist workshops and production space).[8] Although the official opening happened in May 2018, the Democracy circle, of which I was a part until spring 2020, is continuously facilitating the enactment of a horizontal, self-managed organizational structure for Building 7.

Political Practices

From its inception, the ASC enacts "an organisational philosophy based on decentralisation and autonomy; that is, direct democracy, self-management, self-organisation, hinging on individual and collective responsibility."[9] This political project is not about taking political power through the electoral process, but about experimenting in the here and now with political practices/institutional arrangements that enable people who are affected to control their own destinies.[10] True to the principle of self-determination, those active in the ASC invent organizational structures, experiment with them and adapt them on an as-needed basis. The open general assembly that worked well during the first few months, morphs into a spokes-council model as the structure evolves into a loose federation of autonomous projects. Each project has its own mission—popular education, café-bar, itinerant-cinema, media, free bike, and "digestive-tract" (food-related)—and is self-managed by its members. During this phase of intense mobilization and outreach to others in the community, delegates from each of these projects meet at the spokes-council on a regular basis to share, plan, and strategize.

After this, as we focus on the organization of the squat, we return to the general assembly, but this time it is not open to all. It regroups those involved in the autonomous projects and others who agree with the principles of the ASC and want to participate in the opening of the squat. During the campaign to expropriate Building 7, different people are chosen, on a rotating basis, to be our delegates to the *Collectif 7 à nous*. Delegates have enough experience with the ASC to be able to participate in certain decisions without having to get an explicit mandate. It is expected, however, that any decisions that the delegate thinks will generate debate be discussed in the general assembly.

Like the autonomous movements described by Katsiaficas (2006), whatever the organizational structure of the moment, decisions are made by consensus and internal mechanisms are put in place to manage power dynamics. These include speakers lists (first, second turn) to make sure everyone has a say, hand signals to improve efficiency, speaking in "I" statements, vibes-watching, as well as check-ins and check-outs which create space for people to share their emotions and for conflicts to be named and later resolved. Marina Sitrin's analysis applies here. She explains that:

One of the many reasons that *horizontalidad* is not only so powerful but is being used by millions around the world, is that it is a form of making decisions together that is based on each person speaking and listening: it is a politics of listening without judgment rather than creating power over one another. (2012: 70)

Cultural Practices

Horizontal structures and facilitation mechanisms are necessary but not sufficient to enable the emergence of non-authoritarian social relations and different subjectivities. ASC activists were sensitive to the fact that each of us, anti-authoritarian or not, has been socialized in a differentiated and stratified society, and must therefore engage in a conscious effort to get rid of the "master's tools" (Audre Lorde) and replace them with ways of being, thinking, and doing that subvert authoritarian tendencies. Understanding that collective autonomy is an ongoing cultural process, the ASC also experimented with alternative educational, media, and kinship practices.

Education

Both Sitrin (2012) and Zibechi (2010) stress the centrality of *formation* to movement strength and longevity. In order to share its political stance with the most people possible, both the pop ed autonomous project and the *autoformation* committee organize trainings that are open to the general public. Workshops are organized on the history of community organizing in Pointe-Saint-Charles, Parecon (Participatory Economics), collective transportation, squatting, but also, following the solidarity imperative (Katsiaficas), the struggle of the Tyendigaga community against the CN and on direct solidarity with resistance struggles around the world. Internal trainings for members include workshops on emancipatory economic processes, strategic planning and organizing 101. In addition to those types of more formal training moments, the ASC put in place mechanisms for knowledge/skill sharing/learning such as accompaniment for new members, task rotation, and twinning of a more experienced with a less experienced person on a specific task. ASC members refine decision-making processes by experimenting non-authoritarian forms of leadership and by trying to reduce dominating behaviours. To decentralize access to information, the ASC produces a certain number of tools, including a guide, which includes its principles and code of conduct.

Media

Autonomous movements the world over are critical of mass media and put great effort into self-representation (Jeppesen, Lakoff & al. 2014; Katsiaficas 2006). The ASC is no exception. Since it was happening before the widespread use of cell phones and social media, the *médias libres* project invested a lot of time in setting-up media production infrastructure equipped with networked computers and audio-visual materials, as well as a portable antenna that could capture internet signals in different strategic spots in the neighbourhood (which was meant to aid the squat). Moreover, ASC members were constantly disseminating information to sympathisers and the public through various means like the production and distribution of flyers, brochures, and zines during events; plastering the neighbourhood with posters; graffiti; blogging; publishing on the Indy media website (CMAQ) and email blasts.[11]

Media activists also produced a series of short documentaries to use for mobilization purposes,[12] but also to use in our media strategy during the Seracon squat.[13] This media strategy was well thought-out and collectively planned:

> Given the nature of our project, and in order to protect ourselves from mainstream media's tendency to misrepresent [activist actions], we prefer to interact with alternative media. In the event that media coverage is biased, it will be possible to respond effectively by referring to publications produced by alternative media. In order to foster coherence and boost the integrity of our message, a committee of spokespeople will interface with the media.[14]

This committee prepared a cue card so that the different spokespeople could become familiar with the message and be better prepared to face often hostile mainstream media.[15] They produced a video report to share the story of gentrification in Pointe-Saint-Charles,[16] our public declaration, and our critical stance towards mainstream media.[17] Against stardom, and to highlight the collective and horizontal aspect of the squat, the five spokespeople wore colorful carnival masks. The media strategy was effective. Mainstream media wanting to cover this "sensationalist" story had to abide by these rules, and the DIY photos, audio, and video reports circulated widely.

Kinship

> We need folks who are motivated, versatile, who are sick and tired of interacting in a patriarchal, capitalist, racist society that is voraciously materialistic. We want social relations that are rich, egalitarian, that allow us to meet our basic needs, our desires in love, friendship, culture, and art.[18]

The personal is political in the ASC, and efforts are made to create safe(r) spaces that are welcoming, respectful of difference, and accessible for all. We eat together, we take care of the kids, we talk about our personal lives, we fall in love, we party. We share beautiful moments as well as conflict and intensity. We try to be in tune with each other's needs and desires. We build a sense of belonging: a group of friends, roommates, an affinity group, a crew, an intentional family. The ASC is built on relations of trust, attention, and mutual responsibility, or *politica affectiva*:

> The new subject is the new person formed as a part of these new relationships; a subject grounded in *politica afectiva*—a politics of affection, love and trust. Along with this new individual protagonism, a new collective protagonism arises with a need for new ways of speaking of *nosotros* ("we/us"), and *nuestro* ("our") as these relate to *yo* ("I/me"). This aspiration is a genuinely new conception of the individual self through new conceptions of the collective. These new relationships, compelled by the notion of dignity, are the measure of success for these revolutions. (Sitrin 2012: 11)

This is not naïve pretense that all is hunky dory. This is about making visible the cultural processes enacted in the here-and-now that contribute to the expansion of kinship relations that break with authoritarian norms.[19] Also these types of relations bind us together, they are the cement that holds together the spaces we build, where we dare be ourselves, and that feed the courage sustaining us through thick and thin and over time.

Economic Practices

For the ASC, collective autonomy is also about subverting the economy, that ensemble of activities people engage in to produce and distribute goods and services they need to survive (Gibson-Graham et al. 2013). The conceptual tools developed by J.K. Gibson-Graham are particularly well suited to demonstrate how, at a local scale, the ASC contributes to the emergence of a political economy based on economic self-determination (Gibson-Graham 1996, 2006). They suggest that the post-capitalist project is about enacting community economies, those spaces "of decision making where we recognize and negotiate our interdependence with other humans, other species and our environment" (Gibson-Graham et al. 2013: xix). They propose five coordinates to guide ethical deliberation around a diversity of economic practices that are compatible with socially just and ecological livelihoods: taking back enterprise, work, transactions, property, and finance.[20] In this section, I show how the ASC engages in this process of recognition and negotiation, and, in doing so, becomes a community economy.

Taking Back Property or Commoning

In a community economy, enclosed or unmanaged property, irrespective of its legal status, can be "commoned" (Gibson-Graham et al. 2016). Instead of framing commons as a "thing" associated to public or open access property, always subjected to enclosure, these authors suggest that we open up the horizons of possibility in the here-and-now by conceptualizing the commons as a process. Following this reasoning, the verb "to common" refers to those conflictual relations amongst humans, and between humans and the more-than-human world, with respect to these things, material and immaterial, specifically with respect to access, use, benefit, care and responsibility. In addition, it is through this process of commoning that community—or what I refer to as commons-community—is created, self-constituted (Gudeman 2001, cited in Gibson-Graham et al. 2016).

Commoning is at the heart of all ASC activities (Kruzynski 2020): "We believe that it is entirely legitimate and even essential to occupy, renovate and use existing buildings to meet the needs and aspirations of the community."[21] By squatting a factory that was to be transformed into condominiums, the ASC pried open public access to that private property. During the 24 hours that the squat was tolerated by officials, the members negotiated its use and took care of it. Today, only half the site is condominiums, the other half is a public park. A half-victory then. Similarly, during the campaign to expropriate Building 7, the ASC again created the conditions for public access to enclosed private property by organizing mini-squats on the site: sugaring-off (making and distributing maple syrup lollipops), BBQ, public market, movie screenings, to name a few.

By opening these spaces of autonomy, the ASC resisted enclosure, and in doing so built up a counter-power vis-à-vis municipal authorities and capitalist developers who had claimed the site to make a profit. The authorities oftentimes did not know which leg to stand on; they were constantly having to react to a determined and unpredictable adversary who did not hesitate to use direct action to reclaim the site (La Pointe libertaire 2013). Over time, municipal authorities came to tolerate the commoning as practiced by the ASC, as the following anecdote relates:

> The councillors, following the Mayor's request, granted a permit to the ASC for occupation of space at B7... In a conversation with the Mayor, an ASC spokesperson said they did not want a permit. The Mayor retorted that he is aware of the ideology of the centre and that he even told the police chief that "it is not in their habits to ask for a permit, especially when, according to them, the property belongs to them."[22]

With time, our neighbours came to feel "at home" in many of these spaces, Building 7 at the forefront. Through these moments of collective appropriation of property, people were "learning to be affected," a shift in subjectivity that is essential to the emergence of a "commons-community" (Gibson-Graham et al. 2016).

This commons-community has also been consolidated by the multitude of charrettes, assemblies and popular urban planning events organized over the years; in doing so, spaces of ethical deliberation were created in which access and use for Building 7 were discussed and agreed upon. At the heart of these discussions was the preoccupation that the benefits of use be distributed in ways that took into account the wellbeing of all neighbourhood residents, but also the environment. The commons-community, knowing that our neighbourhood is a food and cultural desert, and an urban heat island, developed plans for culturally and financially accessible local services, cultural activities, food production, and green space, to name a few.

Taking Back Work, or Surviving Well Together in Equality

In a community economy we take ethical action by acknowledging how our survival relates to other people and the environment. Surviving well is about "the combination of our love for what we do each day, the quality of our relationships, the security of our finances, the vibrancy of our physical health, and the pride we take in what we have contributed to our communities. Most importantly, it's about "how these five elements *interact*" (Rath & Harter 2010, cited in Gibson-Graham et al. 2013: 21). It is about creating the conditions to experiment and value different forms of labour, achieving a balance that feeds personal well-being—material, occupational, social, community, and physical—without hindering planetary well-being or the well-being of other people.

Understood as a space of "solidarity and mutual aid," the ASC is about the "construction of relations that aim to abolish exploitation in all its forms (human-human, human-nature, other?)."[23] There is an explicit critique of the capitalist practice of wage labour, a valuing of household tasks and a conscious effort to engage in non-capitalist forms of labour, namely volunteering and self-provisioning. There are also debates about inequalities that exist within the ASC. For example, some people have more time to engage in this type of labour because they enjoy excellent material well-being, while others have less time because they are forced to work full-time at minimum-wage and/or cannot count on support from a network of friends/family. Members thus made an ethical decision that complicates the ideological stance for the prioritization of non-capitalist labour practices. Once Building 7 opened, a diversity of labour forms would be available, including wage labour. We would also set up mutual aid practices, such as providing support to those who cannot afford to be properly housed.

There is also a conscious effort to share/rotate tasks that are oftentimes taken on by women, namely domestic and caring labour. During our itinerant phase, the ASC always makes sure that childcare is collectivized. Similarly, at the beginning, the autonomous project Digestive-Tract made the food, and later this task was decentralized with different teams taking it on at different times. Without a doubt, the socialization of housework enabled women to take on interesting and visible tasks that are most often executed by men. A poignant example is evidence of this: two women, each with a baby on her breast, facilitate an assembly of the 80-plus commando on strategy and tactics for the squat.

Taking Back Markets: Encountering Others

In order to take back markets, J.K. Gibson-Graham encourage us to experiment and expand with the ways we exchange goods and services, so that we break with the alienating logic of supply and demand inherent to capitalist markets. They encourage a diversity of transactions/encounters with others that take into account the needs of the people/organizations at the receiving end of the transaction, but also those of the producers and of the planet. These types of encounters are more transparent and are based on the understanding that our survival is interdependent with that of other humans and the natural environment.

The ASC is clear about its position on this matter: "the ASC aims to reframe the relationship between production and consumption (get rid of the culture of blind and irresponsible consumerism)."[24] From its inception, most of the ASC's transactions are gift-based. People are invited to make a voluntary contribution to participate in ASC events. In addition, following the principles of "salvaging, upcycling and creative use of energy sources,"[25] the ASC has developed relationships with local merchants who set aside "ugly" food for pick-up. ASC members also do not hesitate to dumpster-dive containers in public markets and in the parking lots of large grocery chains (a transaction qualified as theft in the capitalist mindset). Gleaning takes time, but reduces the cost of buying food, and, at the same time, it salvages food wasted by capitalist market processes. For example, during Reclaim your Point, the ASC fed 500 people over a 2-day period, for a total of $89.07.[26]

In addition to gleaning, the ASC has established protocols with allied organizations who share their means of production with us, enabling us to DIY instead of renting or buying what we need from capitalist markets. We produce promotional materials using the silk screening and button machines at the Ste.

Emilie Skillshare; we print posters and flyers on the colour photocopy machine at QPIRG-Concordia or AFESH;[27] we borrow the sound-system from Café Paradox to produce concerts; we brew beer for events in a local underground brewery; and we transform food for collective meals in the industrial kitchen at the Club populaire des consommateurs.[28] Similarly, several organizations have gifted products/services to the ASC, including organic vegetables produced by a workers' cooperative or a stand-up comic show by a group of renowned activist-artists.

Although these types of gift-based transactions have been flowering over the years, we are keenly aware that we cannot depend on them for the long-haul. As the ASC projects finally set-up house in Building 7, there is a need to engage in other, more durable, forms of transactions. The ASC is keen on developing encounters with suppliers that are reciprocal, and, when needed, to purchase on ethical markets. As the CSA explains, "imagine a federation of self-managed cooperatives...purchasing supplies from allies—direct (those who we know) and indirect (those who share our ideological stance)."[29]

Reciprocal transactions, based on equivalences negotiated between those involved (Gibson-Graham et al. 2013), might take the form of an alternative currency within Building 7 and eventually beyond, but could also take the form of a local exchange trade system. There is already talk of establishing a protocol that would formalize the transactions between projects within Building 7. For example, organizations within the food production/transformation hub would supply the grocery store Le Detour and the brew pub Les Sans-Taverne; the brew pub would supply other organizations with beer; and producer members of Building 7 could use the woodworking shop and tool library without paying a membership fee.

Taking Back Finance or Investing for Our Futures

Following JK Gibson-Graham, to reclaim the economy for humans and the planet, we need to reframe financial institutions and instruments not as ends in themselves (i.e., the capitalist logic), but as means to enacting better futures. The goal is to find ways for funds to circulate while taking into account individual and collective interests, as well as the health of the planet, and to always consider the well-being of future generations. We must also think outside the box by exploring and experimenting non-monetary forms of investment. We must put forth the time, energy, and imagination to invest in human memory, art, culture, social networks. These types of investments can also circulate, be stored, and amplified.

Investment is a subject of lively debate, namely with respect to investments needed for Building 7 renovations and for the start-up of businesses that the ASC wants to incubate. Mainstream market investment is out of the question, but even alternative market forms of investment—from credit-unions and the state—are considered potential threats to collective autonomy. The ASC creates spaces of ethical deliberation to discuss these touchy issues. Such issues include the pressure organizations feel to engage in capitalist market practices and to expand at all costs in order to reimburse capital to the credit-union, or, in the case of state-funding, the pressure they feel to adopt a legal-status or hierarchical organizational form in order to be eligible for grants, and the perverse effect of professionalization that oftentimes follows.[30] The ASC is not against institutionalization per se, defined as consolidation and longevity, but it aims to avoid professionalization and "the formation of a 'coordinator class.'"[31]

> [These are the] causes and effects of professionalization: lack of rotation and specialisation of coordination tasks; operations become less collective; waning of the political project; wage-labour; difficult access to information needed to make informed decisions; jargon (increased complexity of organisational structures and language); elitism.[32]

In light of this, the ASC considers that non-market and non-state forms of investment are more compatible with collective autonomy. During the first two phases of the ASC's journey, investment took the form of donations as many a student association gave funds and allied organizations donated tools, materials, and infrastructure (e.g. the local reinsertion enterprise Formétal donated bike racks). Anti-authoritarians involved in the collective enterprises to be housed in Building 7 are running socio-financing campaigns and are collecting investments in the form of interest-free loans from the community. That being said, true to its DIY ethic, the most common form of investment is sweat-equity by ASC members and its allies. This is much more than a volunteer contribution. It represents a serious, long-term investment of time, energy, and creativity. As this know-how is invested over the years, it is accumulated and shared with others; in doing so, we are re-investing it in the Building 7 commons-community.

Members of the ASC were keenly aware that once the time came to develop the ASC within Building 7, it would not be possible to depend solely on non-market forms of investment. The ASC thus creates tools to facilitate ethical debates on the matter. The ASC is a ZAF (zone of financial autonomy)[33]—a zone open to the rest of Building 7 and the wider community, but at the same time protected from outside forces "that threaten to derail the ASC from its mission, making it into a social economy project, that is, in the current context, integrated into the logic of capitalist cost-efficiency".[34] Concretely, the ASC has adopted a guiding principle to: facilitate debate on a case-by-case basis and refuse any funding from State, religious, or banking institutions if it comes with strings attached that will constrain the ASC to go against its principles, values, or horizontal organisational form.

Conclusion

Almost two decades later, Katsiaficas's words still ring true:

> As the present world system crashes down amidst us in the next 50 years, we must have a substantive alternative to offer that is a collective creation. In my view, autonomy is that collective creation, and we should study its already existent forms and seek to apply them to our own situation. (Katsiaficas 2001: 555)

The analysis that I have shared herein is one of autonomy, of collective creation, albeit partial and incomplete, as is the revolutionary process. I have chosen to focus on how the ASC invents and enacts subversive practices, without going into challenges, obstacles and conflictual relations that are part of the journey.[35] What this analysis does, is allow us to grasp how the ASC subverts politics, but also culture and economics, by enacting, in the here-and-now a diversity of practices that are coherent with an ethics of self-determination, responsibility, mutual aid and respect for human and non-human others. In this type of revolution, there is no master plan, no grand narrative. The Zapatistas' "asking we walk" provides us with an imaged way of understanding revolution as process (Khasnabish 2010). Following our ethical compass, we walk, together. Sometimes we arrive at an obstacle on the road, or a crossroads. We stop. We take out our compass. We discuss. We decide. We might go on together. We might fight. We might negotiate. We might part ways. We continue.

Today, within Building 7 we are developing a permanent space that will enable the continued subversion of oppressive and exploitative norms and practices in all spheres of life both within the initiative and beyond (Kruzynski 2017). This ethic, these practices, enlarge the spectre of possibilities, as neighbourhood residents and organizations encounter eros, that feisty and energetic force at the heart of the project. Through this process, different subjectivities emerge, norms and values shift, and emancipation becomes possible.

And, importantly, this is happening, simultaneously across the planet. The past 15 years have been marked by a proliferation of economic and political initiatives at the margins of the mainstream (e.g., Alteo 2015; Carlsson 2008; Dixon 2014; Frémeau & Jordon 2012; Grubacic and O'Hearn 2016; Healy 2015; Maeckelbergh 2011; Parker et al. 2014; Sitrin & Azzelini 2014; Solnit 2010; Zibechi 2010). Such initiatives include:

> ...worker, consumer and producer cooperatives; fair trade initiatives; intentional communities; alternative currencies; community-run social centers and resource libraries; community development credit unions; community gardens; open source free software initiatives; community supported agriculture programs; community land trusts and more. (Miller 2010: 25)

These moments of autonomy, of collective creation, are linked together, not by a formal mechanism, but by a web of signification, a process of ubiquity (Gibson-Graham 2006), and, for some scholars, they point towards a large-scale revolutionary shift that is already under way (Graeber 2014).

Endnotes

1 This paper is an adaptation and translation of Kruzynski, A. (2017). "L'auto-nomie collective en action: du Centre Social Autogéré de Pointe-Saint-Charles au Bâtiment 7, " *Nouvelles pratiques sociales, L'action communautaire: Quelle autonomie? Pour qui?,* 29(1) : 139-158.

2 Centre social autogéré de Pointe-Saint-Charles (CSA). (2009). *Vers un Centre social autogéré: Mémoire.* Consultations sur l'aménagement des terrains du CN, Montreal: CSA, p.4, my translation.

3 Some of my comrades commented on earlier versions of this paper, including Marcel Sévigny, Judith Cayer and Margot Silvestro.

4 CSA. (2009). *Déclaration publique d'appui au Centre social autogéré.* Montréal.

5 This is a play on words. Seven (7) sounds like "c'est" which means "it is" and "nous" means "ours," thus: "Collective It Is Ours."

6 Lamont, E (2016). *Le Chantier des possibles.* [DVD]. Montreal: Amélie Lambert-Bouchar and Sylvie Van Brabant (producers).

7 A slogan.

8 Bâtiment 7 (s.d.) *A propos.* Retrieved on 30 May 2017 from www.batiment7.org, my translation.

9 CSA (s.d.). *Principes du CSA.* Montreal. My translation.

10 Because of space restrictions, I focus here on internal political practices. For a detailed analysis of social relations with other actors and institutions, and the building of power, see Kruzynski (2020).

11 A local version of Indymedia, named Centre de médias autonomes du Québec (Autonomous Media Centre of Quebec).

12 CSA (2009), Historique du CSA: https://www.youtube.com/watch?v=1K9UmkX-wHw; CSA (2009). See, by Amy Miller: https://www.youtube.com/watch?v=DzjzEHrr1pw.

13 See, among others: Finalement un centre social autogéré à Pointe-Saint-Charles, CUTV, 2012: https://www.youtube.com/watch?v=fiT7wyw7b1o.

14 CSA (Octobre 2007). *Procédures de groupe : Comité d'installation du Centre social autogéré.* Montréal : l'auteur, my translation.

15 CSA (2009). *Petit pense-bête concernant les relations avec les médias.* Montréal.

16 Centre des médias indépendants. (2009). *CSA message médiatique.* [Web]. https://www.youtube.com/watch?v=bwGxf_2fpzk.

17 Centre des médias indépendants (2009). CSA message médiatique: https://www.youtube.com/watch?v=bwGxf_2fpzk.

18 Margot Silvestro (2012). Op. cit., my translation.

19 CSA. (2011). *Vivre ensemble.* Montréal.

20 I will discuss here only the last four because I did not have access to the deliberations within each of the three businesses that emerged out of the ASC network. These collective enterprises are workers' or solidarity cooperatives.

21 CSA (2009). *Déclaration publique d'appui au Centre social autogéré.* Montreal, my translation.

22 La Pointe libertaire (2013). Op. cit., p.42-43, my translation.

23 CSA. (no date). *Explorer les possibilités quant à l'application de processus économiques alternatifs.* [preliminary working paper], Montreal, p. 6.

24 Ibid, p. 7., my translation.

25 CSA. (2011). *Lignes directrices pour l'ouverture du CSA.* Montreal.

26 CSA (no date). Réclame ta Pointe : Entrée et sortie des bidoux.

27 These are both social justice organizations run on university campuses: QPIRG is the Quebec public interest research group and AFESH is the social sciences and humanities student association of Université du Québec à Montréal.

28 There is no English name for this organization; roughly translates as Peoples' Club for Food Security.

29 CSA, Explorer les possibilités..., Op. cit., p. 7, my translation.

30 CSA—Marcel and Pascal (18 November 2011). *Maintenir et consolider notre culture antiautoritaire (boussole éthique) : en lien avec les impacts du financement de l'État, trouver des mécanismes pour éviter le dérapage.* [preliminary working paper]. Montreal, p. 6.

31 Ibid, p. 3.

32 Ibid, my translation.

33 Referring to TAZs (*temporary autonomous zones*) (Bey 1991).

34 CSA—Marcel and Pascal (18 November 2011). Op. cit., p. 2, my translation.

35 See Kruzynski & Silvestro (2013) for a discussion of challenges and Kruzynski (2020) for an analysis of conflictual social relations and building of power.

References

Alteo, Clifford. (Kam'ayaam/Chachim'multhnii) (2015). Aboriginal Economic Development and Living Nuu-chah-nulth-aht. In Coburn, E. (Ed.), *More Will Sing their Way to Freedom: Indigenous Resistance and Resurgence* (pp. 150-166). Lane Point, Canada: Fernwood Publishing

Ancelovici, Marcos. (2016). Occupy Montreal and the Politics of Horizontalism, in *Street Politics in the Age of Austerity: From the Indignados to Occupy* (pp. 175-201). Amsterdam University Press.

Ancelovici, Marcos, Dupuis-Déri., Francis. (eds.) (2014). *Un Printemps rouge et noir : regards croisés sur la grève étudiante de 2012.* Montréal, QC: Écosociété

Bellemare-Caron, Rémi, Breton, Émilie, Cyr, Marc-André, Dupuis-Déri, Francis, & Kruzynski, Anna (eds.). (2013). *Nous sommes ingouvernables : les anarchistes au Québec.* Montréal, QC : Lux Éditeur.

Bey, Hakim (1991). *TAZ : The Temporary Autonomous Zone.* s. l. : Autonomedia

Breton, Émilie, Jeppesen, Sandra, Kruzynski, Anna, & Sarrasin, Rachel (2015). Anti-racist, Queer, and Radical Feminisms in the Quebec Antiauthoritarian Movement. *Zapruder World: Transformations Without Revolutions? How Feminist and LGBTQI Movements Have Changed the World, 2,* online journal.

Carlsson, Chris (2008). *Nowtopia: How Pirate Programmers, Outlaw Bicyclists, and Vacant-Lot Gardeners Are Inventing the Future Today!.* Oakland, CA: AK Press

Dixon, Chris (2014). *Another Politics: Talking Across Today's Transformative Movements.* Oakland: University of California Press.

Dupuis-Déri, Francis (ed.) (2008). *Québec en mouvements. Idées et pratiques militantes contemporaines,* Montréal, Lux Éditeur.

Frémeaux, Isabelle and John Jordan. (2012). *Les sentiers de l'utopie.* La Découverte, Paris

Gibson-Graham, J.K. (1996). *The End of Capitalism (As We Knew It): A Feminist Critique of Political Economy.* Minneapolis: University of Minnesota Press.

Gibson-Graham, J.K. (2006). *A Post-capitalist Politics.* Minneapolis: University of Minnesota Press.

Gibson-Graham, J.K. (2014). Rethinking the economy with thick description and weak theory. *Current Anthropology, 55*(S9), S147-S153.

Gibson-Graham, J.K., Jenny Cameron & Stephen Healy (2013). *Take Back the Economy: An Ethical Guide for Transforming Communities.* Minneapolis: University of Minnesota Press.

Gibson-Graham, J.K., Jenny Cameron & Stephen Healy (2016). Commoning as a postcapitalist politics. In Ash Amin (Ed.), *Releasing the Commons: Rethinking the futures of the commons.* Routledge

Graeber, David (2014). *Comme si nous étions déjà libres.* Lux éditeur.

Grubačič, Andrej and Denis O'Hearn (2016). *Living at the Edges of Capitalism: Adventures in Exile and Mutual Aid.* Oakland, CA: University of California Press.

Healy, Stephen (2015). Communism as a Mode of Life. *Rethinking Marxism, 27*(3), 343–56.

Jeppesen, Sandra, Anna Kruzynski, Rachel Sarrasin, and Émilie Breton. (2014). The Anarchist Commons, *Ephemera: Theory and Politics in Organisation,* 14(4): 879-900.

Jeppesen, Sandra, Aaron Lakoff, Anna Kruzynski, and Rachel Sarrasin. (2014). Grassroots Autonomous Media Practices: a Diversity of Tactics. *Journal of Media Practice, 15*(1) : 21-38.

Katsiaficas, George (2001). The Necessity of Autonomy, *New Political Science,* 23:4, 547-555.

Katsiaficas, George (2006). *The Subversion of Politics: European Autonomous Social Movements and the Decolonization of Everyday Life.* Oakland, CA: AK Press.

Katsiaficas, George (2011). Eros and Revolution. Presentation at the Critical Refusals Conference of the International Herbert Marcuse Society, Philadelphia, on-line: http://www.eroseffect.com/articles/ErosandRevolution.htm. Consulted, February 11th 2017.

Khasnabish, Alex (2010). *Zapatistas: Rebellion from the Grassroots to the Global.* Black Point, Nova Scotia: Fernwood Publishing.

Kruzynski, Anna (2020). Commoning Property in the City: The On-going Work of Making and Remaking. In Kelly Dombroski & J.K. Gibson-Graham, *Handbook of Diverse Economies* (pp. 283-291), Edward Elgar Publishing.

Kruzynski, Anna (2017). De l'écologie sociale aux économies de communauté : Pour un autre vivre-ensemble. In Collectif, V. Lefebvre-Faucher & M.A. Casselot (eds.). *Faire partie du monde : Réflexions écoféministes* (pp. 53-73). Les éditions du remue-ménage.

Kruzynski, Anna, and Margot Silvestro. (2013). Proximité physique, vie de quartier et luttes anarchistes. In R. Bellemare-Caron, É. Breton, M-A. Cyr, F. Dupuis-Déri & A. Kruzynski (eds.), *Nous sommes ingouvernables : les anarchistes au Québec* (pp.137-151). Montréal, QC : Lux Éditeur.

La Pointe libertaire (2013). *Bâtiment 7 : Victoire populaire à Pointe-Saint-Charles.* Montréal: les éditions écosociété.

Maeckelbergh, Marianne. (2011). Doing is believing: Prefiguration as strategic practice in the alterglobalization movement, *Social Movement Studies, 10*(1), 1-20.

Miller, Ethan. (2010). Solidarity Economy: Key Concepts and Issues, in Kawano, E., Masterson, T., & Teller-Ellsberg, J. (eds.), *Solidarity Economy I: Building Alternatives for People and Planet* (pp.25-41), Amherst, MA: Center for Popular Economics.

Parker, Martin, George Cheney, Valérie Fournier, and Chris Land (Eds.) (2014). *The Routledge Companion to Alternative Organization.* London: Routledge.

Sarrasin, Rachel, Anna Kruzynski, Sandra Jeppesen, and Émilie Breton. (2016). Radicaliser l'action collective : portrait de l'option libertaire au Québec, *Lien social et politiques et RIAC* : un demi-siècle de débats sociaux et politiques, *75* : 218-243. Reprint of article published in same journal in 2012, *68* : 141-166.

Silvestro, Margot (2012). Le Centre social autogéré: une histoire d'expropriation populaire, In *Au cœur de la résistance*, QPIRG Concordia's Working Groups Journal, p.28-29

Sitrin, Marina (2012). *Everyday Revolutions: Horizontalism and Autonomy in Argentina.* NY: Zed Books.

Sitrin, Marina & Dario Azzellini (2014). *They Can't Represent Us! Reinventing Democracy: From Greece to Occupy.* Brooklyn, NY: Verso.

Solnit, Rebecca. (2010). *A Paradise Built in Hell: The Extraordinary Communities that Rise in Disaster.* New York, NY: Penguin Books.

Triollet, Karine (2013). Une décennie de luttes urbaines à Pointe-Saint-Charles : Vers une réappropriation citoyenne. *Nouveaux cahiers du socialisme : Occupons la ville!, 10* : 129-143.

Zibechi, Raúl. (2010). *Dispersing Power: Social Movements as Anti-State Forces.* Oakland, CA: AK Press.

Chapter 7

Decolonization Is Not an Event:
Autonomy, Decolonization, and (Re)Indigenization

Richard Day and Robert Lovelace

Robert Lovelace (RL): On May 13, 1607, colonists arrived in what we now call Virginia. Their interests were to establish a trading colony. The Indigenous inhabitants welcomed them, recognizing opportunity in the foreign goods that the Settlers possessed. The Settlers, some 500, mostly men, assumed that they could be provisioned by the local economy as they waited between infrequent supply ships. None of them possessed Indigenous knowledge or skills. To govern themselves they adopted a class structure that privileged a few while promoting involuntary servitude or idleness among their greater number. Supply ships and the benevolence of their Indigenous neighbours kept them alive for the first 2 winters but following the winter of 1609–1610 only 60 remained alive. Having eaten their way through their boots, the dead from graves, and even excrement, the remaining colonists resorted to cannibalism. There is a lesson for us in this history. While the Powhatans had made living indigenously look easy, the colonists didn't pick up on it. In fact, even while starving to death they were reluctant to understand the fragility of their English manners.

The state of "advancement" that European Colonialism seems to have offered humanity engages many of the fanciful beliefs which the Virginia colonists harboured. However, when today's human population is placed on realistic actuarial scales, what we see as unavoidable are two divergent themes. While technological invention accelerates cultural change, larger portions of the global population suffer poverty and displacement. Those who benefit materialistically with cultural change motivated by advanced technology become more rarified. Privilege is no longer dependent on racial, ethnic, or other inherited markers because technological culture now supersedes all cultures that have any connection to either social or genetic forms of indigeneity. In short: natural economy, slow economy, stable state ecology, indigeneity, whatever the current expression, must become an intentional transition from modernity to something unknown; an existential act within our place in nature. No one knows how to do it.

Technological culture has made careful use of the tools of colonial power which the nation-states have provided. Globally, national governments still define spheres of influence and even battle over them, but only as caretakers at the behest of more organized and efficient corporate interests. Ecological and natural replenishment cycles, manipulated by national legislation, have become assets that corporate players exploit to prop up the illusion of statehood or national paternalism. Living indigenously therefore must be an act of insurrection. Living within a land relationship other than ownership or license is insurgency.

There is no escaping the either/or reality of being a true outlaw or being compliant with colonialism and complacent in a system of eternal alienation. In short, it is the choice between learning how to get along with each other while caring for the land, or eating each other and destroying the land.

Richard Day (RD): Hence the question we want to address in this chapter: How can Settlers and Indigenous peoples work together, for greater autonomy and long-term sustainable thriving, here and now? As Bob says, no one knows precisely how to do this. But many people are working on it, including each of us, in our daily lives, in our teaching, and in our writing.

Here, we will explore this question in the context of George Katsiaficas' book, starting from how he understands decolonization and autonomy. As a counterpoint, and to extend the discussion to explicitly engage with settler-colonial contexts, we will engage with the highly influential and challenging work of Eve Tuck and K. Wayne Yang, via their article "Decolonization Is Not a Metaphor." We will suggest that, in addition to not being a metaphor, decolonization is also not an "event," in the sense of something that can happen, at a particular place and time—something that can be "done" or "achieved." Rather, decolonization needs to be understood as an infinite horizon—a place we might approach, but can never reach.[1]

Also, in response to Tuck and Yang's critique of what they call "Settler Moves to Innocence" (SMTIs), we will note that there are many situations in which Settlers and Indigenous people work together that display at least *some* elements that are not *purely* SMTIs. This happens while working together on the land, while defending, caring for, and restoring the land, and while fighting to return the land to its original keepers. So, while we agree that pretty much anything a Settler does can be seen as an SMTI (i.e. as an act that perpetuates colonization) we would say that some things a Settler might do can also be seen as a Settler Move to Autonomy (SMTA), where autonomy is understood in a way derived from the Two Row Wampum Model.[2]

This leads us to suggest that, while there are strong reasons to deploy an understanding of indigeneity that is based on a combination of ancestry and access to cultural teachings (e.g. avoiding being swamped by unwitting/badly intentioned Settler "allies"), there is also some room for Settlers to take a place-based approach, in situations where this is desired by the Indigenous people of the land they are occupying. This is what Bob articulates as "reindigenization," an ethical (contingent, situated, contested) rather than a moral (fixed, universalizing, always already decided) approach to decolonization and autonomy, for Indigenous Peoples and Settlers, each according to their complex, differential positionings.

Autonomy and (De)colonization in The Subversion of Politics and Resurgent Indigenism

RD: Katsiaficas' book is about European autonomous formations, with a focus on the 1960s to 1990s, so it may seem like a category error to try to engage with his book from the perspective of decolonization practices on the territories claimed by the US and Canadian states today. But Katsiaficas does talk about "decolonization," and he does explain how the European model of autonomy might be generalized, so it is reasonable to assume that these interventions could be relevant to settler colonial societies. Indeed, while Katsiaficas cautions that there is not "one true form of autonomy" (8), he suggests that there are some principles, some commonalities, amongst groups he would call autonomous, that do provide some guidance.

At the level of goals and strategies, Katsiaficas notes that autonomous groups "seek to change governments as well as everyday life" (8), working both within the system and in opposition to it (13). They offer alternatives to both mainstream capitalism and mainstream socialism (8), and they seek to "break the stranglehold of uniformity and integration into consumer society" (14). They are independent of political parties and trade unions (7) and, of course, they do not seek state power. Their success is instead determined by "a capacity to *limit* the powers of nation-states and to create free spaces" (5). Through all of this activity, they transform "what is normally understood as political" by seeking to "expand democracy and to help individuals break free of political structures and behaviour patterns imposed from outside" (6).

In terms of tactics, autonomous groups prefer direct action (11) and militant confrontation (8, 11). Their modes of organization tend towards self-management, non-hierarchical processes of decision-making, and direct democracy, which is in keeping with a high valuation of individual autonomy (8). They believe in "diversity and continuing differentiation" (8), at the individual level and amongst different groups (212). The basic goal of autonomous communalism is to "obviate the need for centralized bureaucracies and giant nation-states by devolving power directly to people affected by specific decisions" (211-12).

This is, of course, a very terse rendering of how Katsiaficas understands autonomy in European contexts, but it is hopefully enough to show that what he has to say resonates in many ways with resurgent Indigenous writers and activists on Turtle Island. Taking up a position that is consonant with the Weberian-Habermasian critique of rationalization of the lifeworld that drives Katsiaficas' work, Marie Smallface Marule and Lee Maracle argued, back in the 1980s and 1990s, that the structures and processes of bureaucracy that are necessary to maintain settler-colonial societies are oppressive as such, regardless of whether they are "imposed" from "outside," or "chosen" from "inside" an Indigenous community (Marule 1984: 40; Maracle 1996: 52). Resurgent indigenists also reject capitalism, which they see as a driver of "outright dispossession, the destruction of land through resource extraction and environmental contamination," and as intricately linked with the colonial state, heteropatriarchy, and racism (Simpson 2014: 13).

Like European autonomist activists, resurgent indigenists shun mainstream political systems and turn instead to direct action. These include "disruptive and confrontational measures" such as reoccupation of Native land, which Glen Coulthard sees not only as effective in blocking the flows of capital and challenging dependency upon the state form, but as prefigurative "in the sense that they build the skills and social relationships (including those with the land) that are required within and among Indigenous communities to construct alternatives to the colonial relationship in the long run" (2014: 166).

The commitment to constructing alternatives to colonial societies also resonates with the European autonomists' lack of interest in achieving state power. In outlining the concept of "anarcho-indigenism," Taiaiake Alfred has advocated for non-statist modes of social organization in which there is "no absolute authority, no coercive enforcement of decisions, no hierarchy, and no separate ruling entity" (1999: 56). This is an outcome that Coulthard identifies as "unfettered autonomy" from, rather than inclusion within, the settler colonial regime (2014: 90).

Although there are many similarities in the ways in which European autonomists and Turtle Island indigenists understand autonomy, there are significant differences in their approaches to decolonization. Following Jurgen Habermas, Katsiaficas argues that one of the main motivators for autonomous movements is resistance to the "colonization of everyday life," which refers to "the penetration of the commodity form into previously private domains and the systematic destruction of the conditions of life" (244). This analysis, of course, is meant to apply only in "advanced western societies," such as those of Europe (244).

The experiences Indigenous peoples have had with colonization are in some ways similar—they involve both of the modalities of invasion described above—but they are, in other ways, quite different from what is described by Habermas. Indigenous peoples have been the targets of franchise and settler colonialism, which involve elements like physical and cultural genocide, removal from the land, and the total, forceful, deconstruction of their lives by people who have come from afar to impose a new life—or death—upon them (Wolfe 2006, Veracini 2010, Mbembe 2003). Thus, although one might say that European state-capitalism "colonizes" its own people, it is important to have greater specificity in our use of this term if we want to theorize the particular ways in which Indigenous peoples have been incorporated into the global state-capitalist system.

Although it is part of the subtitle, and mentioned in the concluding section, Katsiaficas does not extensively theorize the term "decolonization" in his book. It does seem, though, that the term is used in concert with the usage of colonization, i.e., to refer to the "decolonization of everyday life and civil society" (267). That is, it is used in a sense that is also applicable primarily to western societies such as those of Europe. But just as colonization means something different for European societies as it does for Indigenous peoples of Turtle Island, we must respect the fact that people in these two situations also resist and depart from the system in different ways. It is for this reason that many autonomy-oriented Indigenous theorists and practitioners want to reserve the terms colonization and decolonization for talking only about franchise and settler colonialism.

Decolonization and Indigeneity

RL: Before proceeding I need to lay some ghosts to rest. Not to throw cold water on the gentry that live well because others suffer, but I don't think there is an honest discussion being had about "de-colonization." Colonialism in its many forms and political economies does not have an antithesis. There is no opposite to colonialism buoyed by rights-based, democratic, Right/Left moral institutions. These are only cosmetic overlays that accompany denial. Even pseudo-Indigenous identity has for the suffering become a right. But what good is the label when actual lived indigeneity is forbidden and/or forgotten? Struggling to bring down the Windigo only empowers it. An ounce of effort or a smidgeon of time is wasted in following ancestors into the past or exacting violence on "the other side" for a better future. Living well is not dependent on following the "rule of law" or opposing it with moral conviction.

At least 100,000 years have conditioned humans and equipped them to live indigenously. The modern world, except for the slightest epigenetic whispers, is inconceivable in the womb. The womb, that most ancient of floods, is itself an indigenous ecology. The history of all human kind ascends from germination into personality with the sole expectation of being born into a fully indigenous world. Surrounded by others of the closest likeness, the personality seeks rootedness in the soil of community searching with its mouth to swallow connectivity and the most natural sustenance. Arriving under the glare of artificial light must be a supreme disappointment. Being weighed and measured, ranked in size and complexion by strangers is a colossal betrayal. Modernity waits on the doorstep to educate and employ. Nature bows to this insanity because nature is patient.

If we were to understand what indigeneity is, a simple definition that I like to use would be: *A quality of community life having adapted a knowledgeable culture in a specific place where human and ecosystem activity support and enhance one another.* That human infant is prepared genetically to relate to others through a complex system of sensory data simulation and invention with the purpose of collective survival and prosperity. The whole diversity of human kind is descriptive of a fraction of the potential variations in cultural development. A collection of probability and possibility is triggered by interaction with others to form cultural adaptations within symbiotic environments made vital by ecological processes. Humans happen to be the most mobile of communal species, adapting knowledgeable cultures, sustaining themselves on every continent. We have been there and done that.

The dilemma that faces autonomous revolution is that to be successful humans we must re-form communities that are capable of giving birth to our young and caring for our elders. Every successful indigenous culture has mastered this. Within modernity it is the state that has taken this responsibility and left citizens with a moral excuse to abandon it. To assert such a bold undertaking demands an ethical commitment outside of the metropole. Only when a life-long cultural bond based on collective knowledge has formed is it possible to maintain multigenerational continuity. The inherent prescription is precipitous; that is, to move from individual alienation to conscientious unity with others. For the transitory immigrant toward autonomous indigeneity this must begin and end with a willful surrender of the self. On a spiritual level, one must find one's soul.

There has been a significant interest among people of indigenous heritage to learn the language of their ancestors. Like so many other forms of political resistance, speaking a language that only a select few can understand becomes a marker of undisputed identity. But does it bring us any closer to autonomous indigeneity? While the sounds and syntax may have served a successful function for our ancestors in their environments, as servants of modernity it does little else than secure the mask of being the exotic other. One must live in the world of the language to truly understand it.

When Nanabosho, at the dawn of humanity asked, "what is my purpose here," the voice of the creator said, "go out and name all things." Naming was to know, not make up sounds to be assigned randomly to creation. It was this knowledge that humbled the angels when Allah asked Adam to recite them. For indigenous people, knowing where you are, and the specificity of contents and processes is the essential purpose of language. Language is what binds the mind, both communal and personal, to the land; but it is the land itself,[3] the subject of language, and its relationship with humans that is the truth before words. Transitioning toward indigeneity requires the hard work of learning the land and finding and using the words that best communicate it among your people. The words will come if you have knowledge of the place where you belong.

Tuck and Yang: Autonomy, Decolonization, and Incommensurability

RD: Taking aim most proximately at understandings and practices of decolonization in academic discourses of education and the social sciences, Tuck and Yang argue that decolonization is often understood, in these contexts, as just one more "civil and human rights-based social justice project" (2012:2). They are rightly critical of discussions of decolonization that "make no mention" of Indigenous peoples and their struggles for self-determination, and that do not acknowledge "the contributions of Indigenous intellectuals and activists to theories and frameworks of decolonization" (2-3). And, most importantly for this analysis of the relevance of European autonomous theorizing to decolonization in the Americas, they argument that "We are all colonized," may be a true statement but is deceptively embracive and vague, its inference being that "None of us are settlers" (17). As a counterpoint, Tuck and Yang propose an understanding of decolonization that is not about "helping the at-risk and alleviating suffering," but "specifically requires the repatriation of Indigenous land and life" (21). Or, as Leanne Simpson likes to put it, decolonization means "giving the land back; all of it...now" (2015).

While their intervention has brought greater specificity and tangibility to the theory and practice of indigenous decolonization from Settler societies, Tuck and Yang's position raises some questions in terms of how it affects Indigenous-Settler solidarity. Foremost among these is whether decolonization needs to be theorized as a process (something that involves at least partially knowable, if not entirely predictable, changes to an at least partially knowable structure); or as an event (something ineffable, utterly unpredictable and unknowable). At one point, Tuck and Yang note that Patrick Wolfe, upon whose work they rely, argues that settler colonialism "is a structure and not an event" (Tuck and Yang 2012:5), which implies that decolonization would be a process. But there are also passages where Tuck and Yang seem to ascribe a much more event-like quality to decolonization.

For example, in a discussion of *The Last of the Mohicans*, they imagine an alternate outcome in which it is the Settler society that dies out, not the Indigenous one. What is to happen to "the last settler?" they ask? He might leave, "just vanish," or perhaps "ask to stay." These are all questions, Tuck and Yang argue, that "will be addressed at decolonization, and not *a priA ori*" (17). In another passage, they argue that treating decolonization as a metaphor constitutes "a premature attempt at reconciliation" (9), implying that there will be a time of greater maturity when a politics of reconciliation might have greater legitimacy—i.e., the time *after* the eruption of decolonization.

Here, perhaps, while decolonization has been successfully taken out of the realm of metaphor, it has become instead a hoped-for Event,[4] a Utopian horizon, something always to come, but which can never be caused to arrive.

Also, while they clearly establish the goal of decolonization in North American settler societies as repatriation of indigenous land and lives, Tuck and Yang are deliberately unclear about how we might get there from where we are. Invoking Fanon, they point out that decolonization is always "chaotic...and unresolved in its possible futures" (Tuck and Yang 2012: 20). This, in combination with adhering to indigenous protocols of mutual respect and autonomy at all levels, implies that it is simply *impossible to know* how to get to decolonization, in any general, formulaic way, without risking the reproduction of some of the worst excesses of hegemonically oriented, authoritarian settler societies. This implies a lot of people working together, in conflict and cooperation, to constantly adjust what they do, how they do it, and who they are.

To be clear, we do not in any way disapprove of what amounts to a call for autonomous, non-hegemonic, modes of struggle. We are both working, in our own ways, towards the goal of "Native futures without a settler state" (13). Our concern lies with the ethical framework that Tuck and Yang propose as a guide to relationships between Indigenous peoples and Settlers, which they describe as an "ethics of incompatibility." Following from their critique of the metaphorization of decolonization, Tuck and Yang argue that "opportunities for solidarity lie in what is incommensurable rather than what is common" across the colonial divide. The differences that produce the metaphorization of decolonization are, to them, so stark and unmanageable that "lasting solidarities may be elusive, even undesirable" (28). These statements are made, of course, in the specific context of "project(s) of decolonization in relation to human and civil rights based social justice projects" (28). Is it possible to imagine, then, that Indigenous peoples and Settlers *could* work together on projects that don't involve states, rights, and mass-hegemonic approaches to social change? Could Indigenous people and Settlers find ways to work together that are based on autonomy?

If it is true that Settler subjectivity is not something essential and monolithic that resides eternally in certain bodies, if Settler subjectivity exists as a "set of behaviors, as well as a structural location" (p. 7 n. 7), and if decolonization is a process rather than an Event, then some of those who would currently identify/be identified as Settlers could transform their societies (or more likely, survive on the margins and in the cracks while those societies continue to undergo fragmentation), and transform themselves, thereby becoming something else.

Who's Afraid of Eve Tuck?

RL: The problem with considering decolonization as a moral right for some and not for others is that this position gives a free pass, or at least a privileged pass, to a select set of markers, be they skin colour, language, historical marginalization, or state recognition of Aboriginality.[5] From this perspective, for generations of Settler stock and the "poor immigrant," any identification with or work toward decolonization is viewed as illegitimate, as "a move toward innocence." It is an argument that perpetuates colonialism as much as it seeks to offer an alternative analysis. The reality is that there exists a small minority within modern developed Nations who are sick to death with living well because others suffer, and they identify the problem as emerging from colonial domination of labour, the environment and indigeneity. Neither ethnicity nor Indigenous heritage fully defines this group. People come to such understandings through reflexive processes. The folks who identify in this way are more likely to proactively risk the move toward autonomous community regardless of their racial, social, political, or economic markers. They are also more likely to articulate a shared pathway toward re-indigenizing.

On the other hand, speculating whether the pathway toward decolonization is either an event, or process, or "happening," is mere academic clap trap buoyed by the old false binaries dependent on an in-crowd/out-crowd structure. The in-crowd masks its constructed privilege by suggesting that the out-crowd may catch up later if they take a back seat now. And the guilt ridden yet ignorant comply. The academic exercise only reaffirms colonial values of separation and privilege, and for the truly marginalized, leaves them without a functional means of liberation.

Over the twentieth century revolutionary ideologies have convinced us that decolonization depends upon the oppressed making material progress at the disadvantage of their oppressor. We have subscribed to a faith that a critical mass of enlightenment can occur, and people will rise up successfully or evolve peacefully into a utopian understanding of the goodness of mankind. More pragmatic minds like Marx recognized that structural considerations needed to define reality for this to happen. Way before, John Locke believed in the emergence of democratized oligarchs, and, as a man of his time, he also supported himself through investments in the slave trade.

Why do people suffer? Let me count the ways. Each individual sees their own suffering but suspects that after all this time the solution to human suffering remains unknowable. On a macro scale, what we do know is that the earth is experiencing a fairly rapid period of climate change, cheap energy will soon become a rarity for most people, soils without energy to transport nutrients and water will not support present population levels, access to potable water has become a privilege or beyond the economic means of more than half the world's population, and proposed solutions more often than not merely add to the problems. Exacerbating this reality is that control of military power is centered within nation-states that have been predominately insulated from these conditions. One might argue whether this is a process or an event, or whether it can be accountable through apologies or payouts, but in the end it does not matter. Societies argue over refinements in sexual, political, and economic identities while the symbiotic functioning of our ecosystems is collapsing.

Indigenous peoples have been experiencing this ongoing apocalypse for several millennia or more. Many have lost their lives, while some have marginally succeeded. Reindigenization will not be race-based because it does not need to be. It will not be dependent on capital or arbitrary structure. Like indigenous development before modernization, reindigenizing is emergent, responsive to immediate situations and remembered success. In fact, promoting conspicuous markers of identity may well be counterproductive in pursuing adaptations toward autonomous culture.

Eve Tuck has suggested that white people's awakening and/or striving toward decolonization is a move toward excusing the station of their birth. The assumption is that behind every benign Settler personality is a self-serving colonizer. I simply can't envision the world that way. "Moves toward innocence" or moral acceptability are also performed by Indigenous groups essentializing their identities as strategies for survival within modernity. The theology of innocence is a constructed phenomenon among all our social identities. Innocence does not exist in nature, nor does guilt serve anything more than an emotional reminder to check our social behaviour. Guilt, held beyond its natural expiration date, becomes neurosis and counterproductive to its original manifestation. What I see is a streaming mass of humanity heading in one direction motivated by fear and guilt, and the odd individual or small group of no particular history, picking their way through and against the tide. Their opposition is motivated by escape rather than resistance.

Reindigenization is not a romantic vision. Humans only survive, as a species, to the extent that we are able to produce enough offspring to maintain a viable population. The fact that all other hominid species have died out before us does not suggest our success. It really accentuates our potential vulnerability in a non-bipedal world. However, indigeneity is a greater part of our nature. Our vulnerability has been to be conditioned to override our genetic program, the innate ability to adapt as groups within various ecological realities. Moves toward autonomous indigeneity are not motivated by desires for revolution. It might also be argued that escape is not the compelling motivation but rather only the means of leaving an un-indigenous paradigm. The real work begins once we opt out of the colonial/imperial paradigm. Reindigenization is an assertion of our humanity, nothing more, nothing less. It is falling through the sky and upon landing, depending on how we communicate with the natural world around us. It is as Nanabosho, finding himself alone and without purpose asking himself, "What am I doing here? What *should* I be doing?"

Towards An Ethic of Partial Compatibility

RD: Of course, Bob's take on reindigenization could be dismissed as perpetuating, rather than challenging, settler coloni-

alism—as involving nothing more than a "settler move to innocence" (Tuck and Yang 2012: 9 ff.). This is a critique that must
be taken seriously and addressed head on. To do so, we need to
understand who or what a Settler is, and we need to attend to
the thorny issue of the potential roles of Settlers in struggles for
Indigenous decolonization.

One apparently simple, and quite common, definition of a
Settler is: anyone who is not Indigenous to the territory in question. Following this, we must then ask: "Who is Indigenous?"
There are many answers to this question, which invoke factors
like ancestry, culture, language, self-identification, acceptance
by an established Indigenous people, and a commitment to
strengthening and enhancing all these attributes. Given the
complexity and contestation that circulates around understandings of Indigenous identity, it seems that the negative definition
of Settler as "not Indigenous" necessarily suffers from (or is en-
hanced by, depending upon one's politics) a similar fuzziness.

The term Settler can also be understood in a more "positive" way through an analysis of settler colonialism. According
to Tuck and Yang, "Settler describes a set of behaviors, as well
as a structural location" (p. 7 n. 7). Here it is not the purported
qualities of a particular subject that are brought into focus, but
the relations out of which subjects of a particular sort emerge,
and the practices in which they participate. Tuck and Yang also
note that Settler is "eschewed as an identity" (p. 7 n. 7). In the
mainstreams of the Settler societies, very few people want to
take on this subject position, as it reminds them all too much of
who they are, and more importantly, of how they came to be
who they are.

This leads to the question of "Settler futurity," which can be
taken as referring to the structural possibility of living as a Settler as the unknowable processes of decolonization play out as
we arrive at the Event of decolonization. On this matter, Tuck
and Yang are unequivocal. They claim that, "Decolonization
eliminates settler property rights and settler sovereignty" (26);
"Decolonizing the Americas means all land is repatriated and
all settlers become landless" (27); "For social justice movements, like Occupy, to truly aspire to decolonization non-meta-
phorically, they would impoverish, not enrich, the 99%+ settler

population of United States" (26). Here the way in which one understands the term Settler becomes crucial, for if these positionings are taken as referring to Settlers as particular individuals, it seems as though decolonization involves a simple reversal of subject positions, something that Tuck and Yang explicitly say that they want to avoid:

> This is not to say that Indigenous peoples or Black and brown peoples take positions of dominance over white settlers; the goal is not for everyone to merely swap spots on the settler-colonial triad, to take another turn on the merry-go-round. The goal is to break the relentless structuring of the triad—a break and not a compromise. (31)

However, if the term Settler is taken to refer to behaviours and structural locations, that is, if we are talking about subject positions rather than individuals, some of those who would currently identify/be identified as Settlers could transform their societies (or more likely, survive on the margins while those societies disintegrate), and learn to live differently themselves, thereby starting out on a trajectory that leads to occupying a different subject position.

But if this happens, and to the extent that it happens, is it not the case that these people—whatever we might call them—would begin to find that their struggles, as well as their celebrations, would begin to have more in common with those of Indigenous people? And if decolonization is a practical process rather than an ineffable Event, could this not be happening right now? If so, then it seems as though an ethics of incommensurability may not be adequate to guide us, because of the stark line of division it places between Settler and Indigenous subjectivities, communities, projects, and solidarities.

An ethic that might be seen as productively blurring this line—while not erasing it—is advanced in an article by Jeff Corntassel, Rita Dhamoon, and Corey Snelgrove (2014). This piece, which was published in the same journal as "Decolonization Is Not a Metaphor," can be read, at least partially, as a response to Tuck and Yang. Corntassel, Dhamoon, and Snelgrove (hereafter referred to as CDS) argue that, while indigenous and settler struggles are indeed often incommensurable, they are not entirely incompatible (3). This opens up the possibility of "lines of affinity" between decolonization and other struggles (23). Based upon this ethic, CDS do not hold that settlers must become fugitive, landless, and futureless during decolonization. Instead, they argue that "solidarity between Indigenous and non-Indigenous peoples must be grounded in actual practices and place-based relationships" (3).

This is not to suggest that CDS are in favour of massive homesteading operations that would be appropriately challenged under the terms of Tuck and Yang's SMTI number VI. Rather, they say that:

> Just as it is a challenge for Cherokees to be welcomed into
> another nation's territory as strangers, there is an urgent
> need for settlers to change their current relationships with
> the local Indigenous nations on whose territory they reside...
> [T]he impetus is on the settler to change the nature of the re-
> lationship by taking direction from Indigenous nations
> themselves. (17)

In this way, what might be called an "ethic of partial compatibility" allows for the possibility of a decolonizing Settler subjectivity that is radical and place-based; a subjectivity for which every move, of course, contains elements of a desire for innocence and hence involves recolonization; but a subjectivity that can, at the same time, display elements of an authentic commitment to solidarity and decolonization; a subjectivity that can learn from, respect, and be guided by the philosophies and practices of the people whose land it is on. A subjectivity that can be seen as moving towards its own autonomy, while respecting, and contributing to, Indigenous autonomy. As CDS argue, "the ultimate goal is to create the need for a new word or phrase to describe positive features of a settler-Indigenous relationship" (17).

RL: Picking up the tools of survival will be difficult but not as difficult as severing ties of dependency with modernity. It seems to me that this crucial transition carries with it responsibilities for those who immigrate between paradigms. There is always the possibility of bringing disease and corruption from the old world to the new. Even more harmful but more subtle are the unnoticed seeds that accompany us, those invasive species that reduce the complexity of unexplored environments.

Of course, I am writing this as a metaphor as much as it is also an unavoidable reality. It is an unavoidable reality because we do not have the power or wisdom as human beings to avoid inadvertent agency. After all, we are not here on earth for our sole benefit but rather as agents of a greater symbiosis. We do have the insight to imagine ethical responsibility. In my imagination I would like to believe that particular narratives, much like the great floods, fires, and ice of old, will be carried as a warning against the impulse to take too much and to rob our neighbours of what they might have shared freely as acts of mutual benefit.

It is certain that moves toward autonomous indigeneity will focus attention and energy on food security, locally functional technologies, human organization, trade, and self-defence. Success in all of these areas is essential. Mastering these areas requires acquisition and storage of knowledge over successive generations until it becomes "second nature." There is no time to waste, no particular event or sign to wait upon. In fact, there is no perceptible boundary to cross once the journey has begun. The last fire that you will build in the ghostland will be unmarked in time. The road map toward autonomous indigeneity will be signed by meeting your human needs in the real world without depending on the suffering of others. The process is transitional. Today we might be learning to raise food with modern tools while our children may not have such a material benefit. But what we give them is knowledge of food and cultural values, which allow them to value themselves, their family and clan, and the earth that they know.

RD: Our question in this chapter has been: Can Indigenous people and Settlers of Turtle Island find ways to work together that are based on autonomy? Our answer has been yes, they not only can, but they must. If the current dominant order—founded upon the state form, capitalism, racism, patriarchy, and heteronormativity—is not only crumbling, but actively destroying its own foundations; if decolonization is a process, and not an Event; and if it is an ongoing, situated process, rather than an orientation to a Utopian horizon, then there is much that Indigenous people and Settlers urgently need to figure out, here and now. We have suggested that this can and should be done without metaphorization, without reconciliation, but also without privileging incommensurability over the possibilities of affinity.

The Two Row Wampum agreement is often cited as a model of mutual autonomy. But this model suffers from the fact that neither the Settler ship nor the Indigenous canoe are homogeneous. There is plenty of contestation on each side, such that it is often very difficult for, say, a conscientious Settler to precisely interpolate the instructions they are getting from the people whose land they are on. Similarly, Indigenous people can find themselves frustrated beyond all hope and tolerance by the multiplicities and duplicities of the many factions, classes, and other hierarchical divisions that are all too apparent on the Settler side. So, it is quite possible that two rows are not enough, that we need to take an intersectional, N-row approach to Indigenous-Settler relations, without abandoning fundamental respect for mutual autonomy across the colonial divide (Day and Lewis 2015).

George Katsiaficas' book can serve as an important guide for Settlers involved in this kind of analysis and activity. In this chapter, we have noted that there is much in common between European understandings of autonomy and those of resurging Indigenous peoples of Turtle Island. For me, this commonality is not cited in order to argue that "We are all the same" at some level, but rather to point out that there are strong lines of possible affinity between these two traditions. There were, in fact, a number of points in history at which peoples we now see as European related to others currently seen as European in the manner of Empire, i.e., in the manner of variations of what we would now call Settler and Franchise colonialism. And these histories have not been forgotten, as is most obviously and recently evidenced by Irish Republicanism and Catalan separatism.[6] Obviously, the particular characteristics of these struggles are such that there are strong elements of incommensurability and incompatibility between them. But there is enough in common that one can at least hope that they might help to guide Settlers on Turtle Island as we try to transform ourselves into radical, mutually supportive, place-based subjects who know, respect, and take the lead from the people whose land we are on. And yes, if we are privileged enough to "own" some land, by all means, we must work hard to find ways to return it.

Endnotes

1 We should be clear that we believe that all aspirations for social change are of this nature, not just decolonization.

2 The Two Row Wampum (or Guswenta) agreement, struck between the Haudenosaunee and Dutch Settlers in 1613, sets out a mode of settler-indigenous relations that acknowledges the autonomy of both Settlers and Indigenous Peoples, while highlighting the fact that we are traveling the same river together, i.e. that we have common interests, and must address the conflicts and difficulties that will necessarily arise between us.

3 Land, meaning the soils, water, air, climate, all in all.

4 This an allusion to the political event as understood by Alain Badiou, e.g. in *Metapolitics* (Badiou 2005).

5 This term is being used in the sense it is given by Alfred and Corntassel (2005), i.e., as a state-imposed identity, which is explicitly opposed by indigeneity.

6 Here I do not intend to imply that *all* European "ethnonationalisms" can be justified as responses to internal European colonialism. This is an incredibly complex topic that needs a detailed treatment in each specific case.

References

Alfred, Taiaiake. 1999. *Peace, Power, Righteousness: An Indigenous Manifesto.* Don Mills, Ontario: Oxford University Press.

Alfred, T. & Corntassel, J. 2005. 'Being Indigenous: Resurgences Against Contemporary Colonialism.' *Government and Opposition,* 40(4), 597-614.

Badiou, Alain. 2005. *Metapolitics.* New York: Verso.

Coulthard, Glen Sean 2014. *Red Skin White Masks.* Minneapolis: University of Minnesota Press.

Day, Richard and Lewis, Adam. 2015. 'Radical Subjectivity and the N-Row Wampum: A General Model for Autonomous Relations Against and Beyond the Dominant Global Order?' In R. Tafarodi (ed.) *Subjectivity in the Twenty-First Century: Psychological, Sociological, and Political Perspectives.* Cambridge: Cambridge University Press.

Deloria, Vine, Jr. 2003. *God Is Red.* USA: Fulcrum Publishing.

Katsiaficas, George. 2006. *The Subversion of Politics.* Oakland: AK Press.

Maracle, Lee. 1996. *I Am Woman: A Native Perspective on Sociology and Feminism.* Vancouver: Press Gang Publishers.

Marule, Marie Smallface. 1984. 'Traditional Indian Government: Of the People, by the People, for the People,' in Little Bear et al. (eds.) *Pathways to Self-Determination: Canadian Indians and the Canadian State.* Toronto: University of Toronto Press.

Mbembe, Achille. 2003. 'Necropolitics' in *Public Culture* 15(1): 11-40.

Simpson, Leanne Betasamosake. 2014. 'Land as Pedagogy: Nishnaabeg Intelligence and Rebellious Transformation.' *Decolonization: Indigeneity, Education & Society* 3:3, 1-25.

_____. 2015. Talk at Queen's University: 'Islands of Decolonial Love: Exploring Love on Occupied Land.' March 26, 2015.

Tuck, Eve and Yang, K.Wayne. 2012. 'Decolonization is not a metaphor.' *Decolonization: Indigeneity, Education & Society* 1:1, 1-40.

Veracini, Lorenzo. 2010. *Settler Colonialism: A Theoretical Overview.* London: Palgrave.

Wolfe, Patrick. 2006. 'Settler colonialism and the elimination of the native.' *Journal of Genocide Research* 8(4), 387–409.

Epilogue
The Subversive Power of Collective Autonomy

George Katsiaficas

Riding the wave of populism's revival, Donald Trump insists that his promotion of "America First" will lead to a new century of US global hegemony. Although he understands populism as ascending nationalism, I question whether it is simply that. For many people, it certainly is. Aspirations for local self-determination and direct democracy intermingle with ethnic chauvinism. Initial accounts characterized the French *gilets jaunes* (yellow vests) as racist, yet more recent reports have told of a multicultural mix of protesters including many from the *banlieue*.[1] Like many insurgencies since 1968, the yellow vests refuse to name leaders and insist upon open assemblies for decision-making.

Grassroots movements have recently been on the upswing in many countries (evidenced by elected right-wing governments in Hungary, Poland, Brazil, and the US). They reveal racism and patriarchal chauvinism but also the de-legitimization of megalithic political and economic structures. "Populist" direct actions oppose global corporate domination and unprecedented levels of immigration caused by wars fought by militarized nation-states. Trump believes populism's international emergence signals continuing American global domination, but it also portends the demise of nation-states, of their devolution to smaller entities as a world-historical transition to direct-democratic forms of governance takes place. Are people thereby asking for strong central authorities or transitions to more reasonably scaled and democratically controlled decision-making?

More than 30 years ago, devolving Europe and the notion of bio-regional governance in North America were consequences of the continuing impact of movements of 1968, which called for decentralization of political power and more power to the people.[2] So obvious was the growing need for regional autonomy that leading movement theoreticians, whether Marxist-Leninist or anarchist, came to same conclusion—that what is needed is some kind of alternative to nation-states. Black Panther Huey P. Newton advocated for "revolutionary inter-communalism" at the same time that anarchist Murray Bookchin called for "libertarian municipalism." The differences between the two concepts are less important than their similarities. Today, as we see Catalan independence move forward with its promise to demilitarize, Kurdish autonomy emerges with an understanding that a Kurdish nation-state is not needed for autonomist control of liberated spaces.[3] Rojava points to our future more than does the racist fringe encouraged by Trump.

Bannon and Trump want to regenerate American patriotism. They echo the American Nazi Party's cry of "America First!" precisely because they understand that the US has fallen prey not only to economically domineering global corporations but also to a planetary consciousness that rejects environmental devastation in the name of the fossil fuel industry's profits. Trump and Bannon's nationalism is the last gasp of a morbid political system that emerged only a few centuries ago, one that may be destined to last an even briefer period of time than the millennia during which human beings cooperated through forms of governance by assemblies and republics in city-states. No matter how much Trump and Bannon insist that their revival of nationalism will mark the next century of human political endeavor, I believe that planetary relations and technological advances have left the nation-state as an outmoded social relationship, one that is doomed to disappear in the coming centuries—if not sooner.

We can only hope that nation-states will die relatively peaceful deaths. Sadly, countersigns indicate that this process will be anything but non-violent. Look at the million people killed by the dying French Empire in Indochina, to say nothing of the million more lives wasted by French intransigence in Algeria. What can we say about the American genocide in Korea,

Vietnam, and Iraq which lead to the deaths of at least eight million people? We may hope that militarized nation-states, armed
to the teeth with weapons of mass destruction, will gradually
fade away rather than destroying the planet along with their
outmoded political structures.

Since 1970, when Vietnamese leader Ho Chi Minh was
found to be more popular on US college campuses than the
president of the United States, patriotism in America was dealt
a deathblow from which it has only partially recovered.[4] Nationalism's current revival may be embraced by a sizable
minority, but dreams of regional independence increasingly
animate popular movements. From Catalonia to northern Sri
Lanka, southern Thailand to Palestine, Chechnya to Kurdistan,
peoples locked out or enclosed rise up. The former Soviet Union splintered into 15 countries. Many people feel it is time for
California to leave the US, for a variety of peaceful "nations" to
emerge from the militarized American nightmare.

Whether "right-wing" or "left-wing," people increasing
question the obsolete political structure built around majority
rule in elections that seldom offer more than the choice
between Coke and Pepsi. People want direct community control and more democracy—values embodied since 1968 in
European autonomous movements in the 1980s and 1990s and
throughout the world in a series of short-lived insurgencies.
The dying carcasses of the industrial revolution and capitalism,
of patriarchy and hierarchy, are everywhere contested.

Newly emergent tendencies, even when nipped in the bud,
reappear in the aspirations and narratives of human beings
who have freed themselves from the illusion of their own insig-
nificance. Centuries of freedom movements empower and inform present struggles. Women and men of the twenty-first
century are everywhere aware of the lethal impact of mega-
governments and behemoth corporations. Already grander
than ever before, the concentration of wealth in the 1% is accelerating, thereby bringing closer its eventual confiscation by
regional federations of farmers, workers, and ordinary citizens.

Everywhere, younger generations are more loyal to their
cell phones than they are to their governments. They enjoy the
privileges and rights of living in some of the wealthiest societies

in history, yet they also understand that the billionaires who run the world micromanage cities and demand corporate workspaces for the benefit of elites, not the common person. Everywhere the system commands that we work more years at longer hours for less pay.

At the same time as the mainstream media report that socialism is more popular than capitalism among American youth, there is a growing realization that politicians cannot solve problems of climate change, accelerating inequality, and the drudgery of work. People increasingly recognize that the corrupt system of militarized nation-states ruled by parliaments of, by, and for billionaires and demagogues is the problem. While we may welcome Bernie Sanders' efforts and cheer the new generation of progressives in Congress with their Green New Deal, the political system's incapacity to solve key problems is already evident. There was never a vote on the Vietnam War or the Iraq Wars, never a referendum on nuclear power or the massive subsidies granted to the automobile industry in the form of trillions of dollars expended on highways; never a popular mandate for destruction of neighborhoods to build freeways. There has never been a popular mandate for the 1% to "own" the vast social wealth created by generations of toil and sacrifice.

The essays collected here are concrete evidence of the intergenerational robustness and significance of autonomous movements that reject participation in mainstream politics. The history of social movements, sometimes savagely repressed and nearly exterminated as in the case of Korea in the twentieth century, also reveals the continuing reemergence of very specific issues and aspirations that animate struggles. The ideas developed by activist intellectuals in the preceding essays have far advanced my own thinking in *Subversion of Politics*. Even more significantly, social movements themselves have re-invigorated the concept of autonomy in such groups as Black Lives Matter, whose organizational structure is built around independent regional decision-making. Black Lives Matter (BLM) provides evidence of how local groups seek to regain control of alien political and military forces and to build grassroots democracy. Although BLM may appear to be quite different than the Black Bloc or German Autonomen, their essential characteristics converge in rejection of mainstream parties while building direct-democratic forms of power. Apparent differences between First Nation activists and the radical progeny of European settlers is a theme addressed by Richard Day and Robert Lovelace in this anthology. They discuss the differences between "decolonization" advocated by oppressed people and the meaning of "decolonization" for autonomist movements in advanced capitalist societies. Day and Lovelace conclude that "European understandings of autonomy and those of resurgent Indigenous writers and activists on Turtle Island" have much in common.[5]

Reading through the essays collected here, four streams of thought have come to mind:

Individual and Collective Autonomy

Before the emergence of the European Autonomen, discussions of autonomy in the European or western context would have involved the notion of *individual* autonomy. Today, understandings of collective autonomy have transformed traditional European comprehension of autonomy as primarily a concern of the individual.

In her analysis of anti-authoritarianism in Quebec, Rachel Sarrasin traces the shift from Kantian individual autonomy to its collective forms. She finds that, "at the core of the collective autonomy project of the anti-authoritarian community ... lies ... the idea that people involved in a specific situation are best located to collectively determine their needs and how they wish to function." Their notion of an anti-authoritarian community involves workers' cooperatives developing the practices of economic self-determination, efforts they understand as needing to be supplemented with autonomous movements' capacities to overcome gendered and racialized social relations. Their ideas are derived from experiences such as mobilization by the *Centre social autogéré* in the Pointe-Saint-Charles sector of Montreal against gentrification as well as the creation of intentional families among queer and trans people of color. As an aside, I note that several of the essays here grow out of Quebec's practical development of the autonomist project. All too often Canada has been marginalized in American theory and practice, and I hope this book helps to build a more global construction of autonomy in North America.

The innocence with which many of us enter movements and suffer betrayal is a topic for a lifetime of work. Particularly among left-wing social movements do we find a perverse history of internecine assassinations, violent disagreements, and co-operation with the police by those who perceive former allies as rivals. In Germany, an emphasis on individual transformation has become one of the main responses to intra-movement violence. Emiline Fourment discusses women's responses to the problem of rape within the movement and finds women had to take the leading role in seeking to end rape and sexual violence among activists, a fact that should come as a surprise to no one. No oppressed group in history has ever been able to make changes for their benefit in the face of more powerful adversaries, and it is rightful and just that women have used a variety of techniques to confront and punish men whose "orgasm is more important to them than the well-being of their female victims." As she points out, "it was inconceivable for activists that their comrades and friends, with whom they not only had strong ties but also fought for social justice, could assault a woman."

As in society, so it often is inside the movement. Women who made accusations of rape were often disregarded, accused of making false claims, and compelled to recount publicly the details of their humiliation at the hands of male aggressors. Over time, alternative forms of inquiry into injustice have emerged largely due to the passionate and thoughtful involvement of women for whom the issue could not be suppressed.

Fermont traces the evolution of feminist responses from confrontational to pedagogical. When dealing with aggressors, transformation of their individual behavior and personalities became an essential part of movement efforts. Yet Fourment observes that by the end of the 1990s, at the same time as feminist Autonomen had won over the vast majority of the movement to an understanding that all participants' integrity should be protected, the discourse became more academic and theoretical. In the same period of time, movement actions in Germany sharply declined. Fourment believes the contribution of Judith Butler played a pivotal role in rejuvenating feminists' involvement in autonomous thought and actions by helping to move from the early days of confrontation of rapists to more recent attempts to heal and transform perpetrators.

The German movements' strong reaction to male domination indicates that individual rights are being extended to include women's rights to peace and happiness, that collective autonomy is not the simple negation of individual autonomy but its sublation or determinate negation, a recreating of autonomy at a higher level than patriarchal society could attain. The issue is not the primacy of the "individual ego" but of harmonizing the individual with the collective.

In the conference leading to this book, Francis Dupuis-Deri explored ways in which the movement's militancy, glorified in the form of "riot porn," makes rape more possible through a ritualization and acceptance of violence. He criticized left tendencies to ridicule emotion and argued for gender neutrality. Making an important observation, Dupuis-Deri told how the hidden individual identities within Black Blocs make them a gender-neutral zone.

For AK Thompson, the "collapse of the interval between ontology and politics" has had deleterious effects. As activists turned inward, they were cut off from potential bases of recruitment and became isolated. Reading *The Subversion of Politics* closely, he notes that I commented on ways in which "radicals felt that the slogan 'The personal is political' had been turned on its head." As early as 1979, movement publications devoted more space to sadomasochism than the missile crisis which was bringing hundreds of thousands of people into the streets.

Nature within us is a powerful ally, as Marcuse pointed out. Truly revolutionary movements need to transform instinctual structures so that we become capable of freedom. Millennia of obedience to patriarchal rule and subservience to unjust economic structures inherited from the past have left their scars. Rather than resting upon an eternally unchanging view of human nature, Marcuse understood that our internal Nature, like the Earth, is continually changing. The issue is to cognitively determine in which direction we should transform ourselves so that humans formulate a new universality among the species. In the struggle to transform instincts and prepare a genuine revolution, Eros and cognition play paramount roles. The eros effect is our ally in struggle, and in order to activate it, we need to seize control of Nature within us.[6]

In the last three decades, movement concerns in many places have become more defined by the transformation of individuals as part of the wider process of social transformation. Anna Kruzynski discusses a "shift in subjectivity" as essential to the emergence of new "commons-community." She focuses on how Building 7 in Montreal, a free space won from the city after years of struggles, created a context for ethical deliberation and collective consensus on many decisions, including resource allocation. Activists involved in these tasks have made conscious efforts to socialize what has been considered traditionally women's work, i.e., domestic and caring labor. Kruzynski points out that Building 7 grew out of eruptions in Quebec such as the anti-FTAA and anti-war revolts at the turn of the century, Occupy in 2001, and a massive student revolt.

Jason del Gandio's chapter explores his own personal evolution in state-sponsored group homes for children. As a young five-year-old, he was suddenly placed in a temporary boys' home. Without the language or cognitive ability to comprehend what occurred around him, he recalled how some of the boys joyously jumped from bed to bed, awakening him in a:

> ... spontaneous melee of young boys reclaiming their humanity and expressing their displeasure with the home that they did not ask for and could not leave. The moment burns eternal in my mind, The boys glowed in the early morning sun—laughing, jumping, rebelling.

Autonomous Movements and Parliamentary Oppositions

The recent experiences of *Syriza* (Coalition of the Radical Left) in Greece once again clarifies how imperatives of capitalist democracy deform even the most ardent revolutionaries when they choose to work within corridors of national power. Since the rules of the game are that legality must be protected, even when it means disenfranchising millions of seniors on pensions or otherwise contradicting one's principles, *Syriza* proves once again that even the best-intentioned revolutionaries, when they choose to work within the existing structures of political power, can at best only legitimize outmoded forms of governing.[7] Ancient Greek city-states flourished for centuries by continually dividing and creating themselves anew in places like Marseilles and Syracuse. Just as changes in social relations rendered them powerless, historical development has created the preconditions for the obsolescence of nation-states. It is no accident that in this era, Bookchin's municipalism and Newton's inter-communalism were envisioned.

Although autonomy has many definitions, its primary characteristic is to reject political parties that work within established systems. It means to reject militarized nation-states and to work for the destruction of such governments. The Zapatistas refuse to participate in Mexico's corrupt government, a principled position that emanates from the aspiration of actualizing a free society worthy of the name. Autonomy means a "politics of the first person," to articulate for ourselves our needs and aspirations—not those of the Party or leaders.[8]

The traditional left generally accepts Rudy Dutschke's notion of a "long march through the institutions." Autonomous understandings are quite different, emphasizing destruction of such institutions over a long period of time and development of dual forms of power based upon consensus in direct-democratic assemblies. New forms of decision-making are insisted upon by individuals who have liberated themselves from false notions of democracy.

Breaking From the European Notion of a Monocentric Public

Whether observed in Habermas' notion of a singular universal public or Antonio Negri's endorsement of the European Union, traditional left (and not only European) notions of politics essentially assume a single universality. Autonomous social movements seek to reinvigorate a plurality of endeavors and diffuse publics. Sometimes existing in harmony with each other and at other times contradicting one another, autonomous communes reflect the inherent contradictions omnipresent in human existence. Traditional notions of European political theory flatten out such concerns. Negri rejects the very idea of contradiction. Rather than understanding that the particular is subsumed by the universal, autonomous activists understand that the universal resides in the particular. Black music is all of our music. Feminism benefits us all, liberating us from obsolete structures of patriarchal domination.

Central to Marxism-Leninism is a fetishization of the "conscious element" (one leading Party) in opposition to "spontaneity," as well as a rejection of emotion in favor of consciousness. Breaking with such a Cartesian conception, autonomous movements, like Indigenous peoples in ancient Egypt and ancient America, understand a rationality of the heart; we embrace emotional reasonability and applaud freedom-loving impulses. Our global understanding of autonomy necessarily involves leaving behind frozen categories. No longer bound to Eurocentric notions of politics or to western trajectories, new avenues are open for the explorations of redefined forms of governance. Nothing short of extirpation of traditional European forms is required for the rebirth of freedom at a higher level.

The Revolutionary Subject and Autonomous Movements

Karl Marx made lasting contributions to our understanding of economy and society, yet in the twentieth century, reification of Marxist insights has produced an obfuscation of the revolutionary roles played by segments of the population not defined by any occupational category. Working class dogmatism helped to kill the movements of 1968. If we focus on analyzing the actions of millions of people in the past five decades, a very different understanding of the revolutionary subject emerges. It is no use to replace outmoded ideas of the working class and proletariat in the same schematic structure but with a different vocabulary. What is needed is to concretely analyze our specific conditions and to recognize who has been leading freedom struggles. In South Korea, the 99%, self-identified as the *minjung* in the 1980s, led the overthrow of military dictatorships that had ruled since 1945. After Occupy Wall Street, millions of us identified the 99% as the base of change.

Since 1968, the global movement's mobilizations have changed from being spontaneous and unconscious to a form of "conscious spontaneity" in which grassroots activists around the world synchronize protests with common aspirations. Popular insurgencies expand upon preceding struggles and borrow each other's vocabulary, actions, and aspirations. Movements assimilate lessons from previous protest episodes. People improvise tactics and targets from their own assessments of past accomplishments and failures.

In the period after 1968, as the global movement's capacity for decentralized international coordination developed, five waves of international insurgencies can be discerned:

1. The disarmament movement of the early 1980s

2. The wave of Asian uprisings from 1986–1992

3. The revolts against Soviet regimes in East Europe

4. The alter-globalization wave from Seattle 1999 to anti-war mobilizations on February 15, 2003

5. The Arab Spring, the Greek rebellion and the Occupy movement in 2011

In my view, such globally synchronized waves of protest are significant precursors of future events.

At the beginning of the twenty-first century, it was often repeated that autonomous movements had disappeared. No sooner had they been pronounced moribund did they reappear in 2001 in Göttingen and again in 2007 in Heiligendamm at the G8 protests. Although autonomous movements are continually declared to have vanished, they reappear in forms like the Black Blocs in Egypt, Brazil, Mexico, and elsewhere. The Invisible Committee in France follows in the autonomous tradition of rejecting traditional political parties and emphasizing direct action. The *gilets jaunes* have key characteristics of autonomous insurgencies. They refuse to acknowledge any leaders or to participate in hierarchies.

The Making of *The Subversion of Politics*

The Subversion of Politics had its origins in the personal dilemma I experienced as the movements of the 1960s and early 70s gradually subsided. For over a decade, I had given my every effort to opposing war and racism and building community power in a small countercultural community in Ocean Beach, California (OB).[9] Amid intense police, FBI, and right-wing repression, betrayals within the movement set in. OB's vibrant communalism lost its heart. As I pondered my next move, I decided to go to Spain and mentioned it to one of my best friends and mentor, Herbert Marcuse. He laughed. "What are you going to do in Spain?" he asked. "You'll be bored in no time." Answering a question with a question in the kind of Socratic banter we often fell into, I asked him where he thought I should go. "Berlin, of course" was his reply. That conversation is where my involvement with German social movements began.

After arriving in Berlin in 1979, I was fortunate to find roommates who were involved in the struggle against the Gorleben nuclear waste disposal site. I joined with them in those protests. With another friend, I traveled to Amsterdam where the squatters' movement was at its peak, and I was present as the movement spread to Berlin. Upon returning to the United States in 1981, I wrote about the anti-nuclear missile movement, then at its height with hundreds of thousands of people marching against intermediate range missiles (the ones Trump is talking about bringing back) in Rome, London, Paris, and Bonn. While visiting my father (a highly decorated World War II veteran who knew Germany well), he read some of my prose and accused me of perpetrating Nazi-like myths by talking of things that did not exist. Undeterred by his skepticism, I included my writings on Germany in what became my dissertation (subsequently published as *The Imagination of the New Left*).

After I moved back to the East Coast, the Black Rose lecture series invited me to make a presentation on autonomous movements at MIT. No sooner had I begun than I was interrupted by a concerned activist who insisted I was inventing the Autonomen. The Greens, he insisted, were happening in Germany, and if an extra-parliamentary movement really existed, he maintained the media would have been full of stories about them, yet none had appeared.

I included Germany in the 1980s in my dissertation to provide empirical evidence of the world-historical character of the 1960s movement, as a way to counter working class idolaters who insisted the sixties were an aberration, that subsequent movements would be characterized along the lines of those in the 1930s. In any event, I deleted that chapter in the book version to better focus on 1968–1970. *Imagination* was the first book to consider the 1960s as a global movement, confined neither to one country, one decade, nor to race-specific dynamics (and decidedly not focused on individual biographies but on the actions of millions of people).

Years later, I dusted off the long-discarded chapter on Germany, updated it and published it as *The Subversion of Politics* with Humanities Press. Within months of its publication, Humanities Press went out of business, and the book disappeared once again. Over the next several years, encouraged by younger activists, I uploaded the book as a free download on my website (eroseffect.com). I happily noticed unauthorized reprints of chapters at movement conferences, one thanking me for not minding that my work was reprinted—even though they had done so without my knowledge or permission. Luckily, AK Press decided to publish the book once again, and it was subsequently translated in Greece, Russia, Chile, and Korea. In Italy and Brazil, journalists have referred to me as the "father of the Black Bloc" despite the fact that the Black Bloc has no father, nor mother. Despite such false accolades, I am gratified that my ideas have resonated with younger activists and have learned from their expansion of the meaning of autonomy in their own contexts. I especially want to thank Marcos Ancelovici and Francis Dupuis-Deri for organizing this effort to reflect upon the book's relevance twenty years after it first was published.

Ocean Beach, California

December 30, 2018

Endnotes

1 See Robert Mackey, "The Faces and Voices of the 'Yellow Vests' in France," *The Intercept*, https://bit.ly/3GLfYt0, accessed December 28, 2018.

2 *The Global Imagination of 1968; Revolution and Counterrevolution* (Oakland: PM Press, 2018) is a heavily revised and expanded version of my 1987 book, *The Imagination of the New Left: A Global Analysis of 1968* (Boston: South End Press).

3 Abdullah Ocalan, *Democratic Confederalism* (San Bernardino: Transmedia Publishing 2014) makes quite clear the need to overcome the nation state.

4 In contrast to popular wisdom, ideological and sectarian leftists, from the Progressive Labor Party to self-described Situationists, converge in their chauvinistic regard of Ho Chi-minh as a "traitor" to Vietnamese people.

5 At the same time, they rightfully point out that decolonization is a process and not an event. They quote Tuck and Yang to the effect that "Decolonization eliminates the settler property rights and settler sovereignty" so that genuine decolonization would mean "all land is repatriated and all settlers become landless."

6 Together with AK Thompson, Jason Del Gandio edited *Spontaneous Combustion: The Eros Effect and Global Revolution* (Binghamton: SUNY Press, 2018), an anthology in which scholar-activists explore the eros effect from new perspectives.

7 Spain's *Podemos* is young and has yet to achieve the level of support or power which *Syriza* amassed, but the same admonition can be made for any efforts to reform Spanish democracy rather than to break its central power.

8 See *The Subversion of Politics: European Autonomous Movements and the Decolonization of Everyday Life* (Oakland: AK Press, 2006) 6-9 for the meaning of autonomy.

9 See the end chapters of Andre Gorz, *Ecology as Politics* (Boston: South End Press, 1980) for discussion of Ocean Beach.

Biographical Sketch of George Katsiaficas

Born in El Paso, Texas, *George Katsiaficas* grew up in the US Army. By the time he left home to go to college at MIT, he had lived more than half his life abroad, in Germany (Berlin, Frankfurt, and Wertheim-am-Main) and Taipei, Taiwan. In the US, he went to public schools in Brooklyn and Queens, New York, and Baltimore, Maryland, where he finished high school at Baltimore Polytechnic Institute (a public inner city school) in 1966.

From 1969, Katsiaficas has been active in social movements. In 1970, in the midst of the nationwide student strike, he was graduated from MIT while in solitary confinement after being convicted of "Disturbing a School" for organizing antiwar protests. MIT mobilized charges against him using a long-disregarded eighteenth century statute. So egregiously unjust was MIT's targeting of him that even his mother was imprisoned for a week in the notorious Charles Street Jail for objecting to the judge's refusal to allow a witness whose testimony would have cleared him of the charges against him.

After being released from prison, he helped to realize an idea that came to him while in solitary and founded the Red Bookstore (which today survives as Boston's Lucy Parsons Center). Escaping continual arrests and prosecution in Cambridge for his support of the Black Panther Party, he moved to California, where he helped to create a deep network of countercultural counterinstitutions in Ocean Beach, San Diego during the 1970s. Shortly after he moved to California, his collective house was shot up and his car firebombed by the FBI-organized all-Mormon Secret Army Organization. The FBI referred to him in their files as a "New Left/anarchist," and he was classified "Priority 1 ADEX," indicating that he was to be immediately arrested in the event of a national emergency.

In 1972, he moved briefly to Miami, Florida to help organize protests at the Republican National Convention. After returning to Ocean Beach, he cofounded Red House, an activist commune built upon agitating and building counterinstitutions to organize a revolutionary base area in Ocean Beach. Arrested during a shoot-out in which two policemen and one comrade, Peter Mahoney, were wounded, he went on to lead an anti-police movement from 1974 that aligned with Chicanos and African Africans to get the police chief of San Diego fired. He founded another collectively managed non-profit bookstore, the Left Bank, helped to organize a food coop (which today survives as Ocean Beach People's Food Store), and led study groups based upon the writings of James and Grace Lee Boggs. After driving a taxi for several years, he became friends with Herbert Marcuse and enrolled at UCSD, where he was active against the CIA and for Palestinian self-determination. Despite two trials brought by UCSD, he escaped expulsion from graduate school because of overwhelming popular support.

With Marcuse's support, he received a Fulbright Fellowship and enrolled at the Free University of Berlin. In his doctoral thesis, he uncovered the "Eros Effect" to explain the global synchronicity of movements in 1968. His 1987 book, *The Imagination of the New Left: A Global Analysis of 1968* was the first study to comprehend a globally unified uprising among the plethora of diverse social movements that had emerged simultaneously and previously been understood within national boundaries. The Eros Effect portrays how and why social insurgencies simultaneously erupt as much in relationship to each other as to larger economic and political dynamics. He developed the concept to explain the rapid spread of revolutionary aspirations and actions during the strikes of May 1968 in France and May 1970 in the US as well as the proliferation of the global movement in this same period of time as evident in the spontaneous spread of revolutionary aspirations in a chain reaction of uprisings and the massive occupation of public space. No other theory could adequately explain the sudden entry into history of millions of ordinary people who acted in a unified fashion, intuitively believing that they could change the direction of their society. From his case studies, he came to understand how in moments of the eros effect, universal interests become generalized at the same time as the dominant values of society are negated (such as national chauvinism, hierarchy, and individualism). Katsiaficas' 1987 book was the first to discuss how contemporary social movements have changed the world without seizing political power. In 2007 at a conference at Queen's University in Canada, he maintained that despite the relatively quiet period then predominant, protests on a global scale were soon to erupt, a prediction verified by the subsequent Arab Spring, Occupy Wall Street, and Black Lives Matter movements. In 2017, Jason del Gandio and AK Thompson edited a volume of responses to the Eros Effect: *Spontaneous Combustion: The Eros Effect and Global Revolution* (SUNY Press).

For years, Katsiaficas taught at Boston's Wentworth Institute of Technology, a working-class college, during which time he was a research affiliate at Harvard University in both European and Korean studies. After his book on 1968 was translated into Korean and became something of a best-seller, he visited Gwangju for the first time in 1999, where he eventually married filmmaker Shin Eun-jung, whose critical documentary about Harvard won a prize for Best Director of a Documentary at the 2011 New York International Film Festival. In 2007, Katsiaficas was awarded a Fulbright fellowship to Korea, and he lived and taught at Chonnam National University in Gwangju, South Korea for many years. Katsiaficas' research and writings have consistently challenged Eurocentric and traditional approaches to social theory. When writing about movements, his vision is not restricted only to the West. Inspired by the 1980 Gwangju People's Uprising, he spent 13 years of research before completing his two-volume volume book, *Asia's Unknown Uprisings*, which places the 1980 Gwangju Uprising at the center of an Asian wave of grassroots insurgencies that overthrew eight dictatorships in six years.

His second book, *The Subversion of Politics: European Autonomous Social Movements and the Decolonization of Everyday Life* (1997), analyzed post-1968 radical formations in Germany, Switzerland, Italy, Holland and Denmark. Katsiaficas' writing about the German autonomous movement, with its emphasis on revolutionary politics, squatted housing and cultural spaces, and street militancy including black bloc tactics, was influential for many anarchists and other US-based radicals at that time. The protest tactic of the black bloc, for which demonstrators all dress in black, cover their faces, and move as a coordinated group to neutralize police surveillance and attacks, was first used in the US in the early 1990s at the Earth Day Wall Street Action and the DC march against the first US Gulf War. Katsiaficas' work about the Autonomen traces the lineage from 1968 through Italian feminism, the antinuclear movements, and antifascism, to their confrontational politics. He also draws out the (anti)politics and the theory of autonomy from his movement investigations. He conclusively shows how the German Green Party grew out of extraparliamentary protests, and further portrays how grassroots militancy opened space for the huge participation in subsequent mobilizations for nuclear disarmament, the massive protests that opened the door for Gorbachev to relinquish Russian control of Eastern European buffer states once he realized that Germany would not invade the Soviet Union again in the twentieth century. He is critical of Antonio Negri and forms of "Autonomía" that failed to recognize how feminist autonomy preceded and patterned subsequent forms.

Katsiaficas is distinct from many academics in that he has also been a dedicated organizer. He goes beyond participant-observer to militant researcher, someone who lives amongst and collaborates with the people he writes about and sees his research as advancing global activism, not simply describing or analyzing it. This doesn't bias him against abstraction and analysis, however, but rather grounds his theoretical work in struggles to transform the world. His prioritizing *praxis* explains why his theorizing appears at the conclusion of his books, rather than in the opening chapter(s) as is typically the case for academic monographs. It is the history of social and political revolt woven together with his personal commitment to radical politics that enlightens his work. Together with Kathleen Cleaver, he edited *Liberation, Imagination and the Black Panther Party*. His latest book, *The Global Imagination of 1968: Revolution and Counterrevolution* (PM Press), discusses Sixties' movements in more than fifty countries and outlines global waves of uprisings subsequent to 1968. During his international sojourns, he has been active in liberation struggles in Germany, Lebanon, Korea, Greece and other places. Translations of his books have appeared in Korean, Russian, Greek, Spanish.

He was editor of *New Political Science*, 1998-2003, Chairperson of the Caucus for a New Political Science, American Political Science Association, 1989-1991, and founded a book series for the Caucus. He was a central organizer of a 2003 Harvard University conference about the Jeju Massacre of 1948, and in Bangladesh in 2010, he initiated a conference on that country's 1990 uprising. Noteworthy awards he has received include the Kim Dae-jung Scholar's Award (Hu-Kwang Award) at Chonnam National University in May 2016, being made an Honorary Citizen of Gwangju, South Korea, in 2016, the Charles A. McCoy Career Achievement Award for a progressive political scientist who has had a long career as a writer, teacher and activist presented by the Section for a New Political Science of the American Political Science Association in 2011, and in 2010 an award for Outstanding Service from the May Mothers' House (widows and mothers of men killed in the 1980 uprising for democracy in Gwangju). He often participates in meetings of the International Herbert Marcuse Society.

About the Contributors

Marcos Ancelovici is Professor and Department Chair of Sociology at the Université du Québec à Montréal (UQAM). He studies social movements and housing struggles, and has been involved in several antiracist as well as pro-housing and pro-civil liberties collectives. He is co-editor, among other titles, of *Street Politics in the Age of Austerity: From Occupy to the Indignados* (2016).

Richard Day is a political philosopher and former professor at Queen's University, best known for his book *Gramsci is Dead: Anarchist Currents in the Newest Social Movements*. He is currently living at The Snag Farm on Denman Island BC, which is the home of the Denman Centre for Alternative Living and Learning (D-Centre). His work there is focused on building and sharing skills for autonomous, community-based subsistence in these challenging times of climate change, war, and political-economic upheaval.

Jason Del Gandio is an Associate Professor of Communication and Social Influence at Temple University (Philadelphia, USA). He specializes in the theory and practice of social justice and the performance, philosophy, and rhetoric of liberation. He's published four books and numerous essays for both scholarly and popular venues. He was part of the global justice movement, the anti-war movement, and the Occupy Wall Street movement; he traveled to Venezuela to observe and report on the Bolivarian revolution; he worked on Latin American solidarity campaigns; and he taught a class on social movements in a state prison. He believes in the liberation of all people, of all places, of all times.

Francis Dupuis-Déri teaches political science and feminist studies since 2006 at Université du Quebec à Montréal (UQAM), published several books in French, some being translated in English: *Who's Afraid of the Black Blocs: Anarchy in Action Around the World* and *Anarchy Explained to my Father* (with Thomas Déri), and edited (with Benjamin Pillet) the collections of interviews *Anarcho-Indigenism: Conversations on Land and*

Freedom. He has been involved in anarchist style collectives in Québec, France and the United States.

Émeline Fourment is Associate Professor in Political Science at the Université de Rouen Normandie (France) and a feminist anti-authoritarian activist. Her research deals with women's movements, health movements, gender-based violence, and critical criminology in comparative perspective (Germany, Québec, France). Her doctoral dissertation examined various appropriations of feminist theories (materialist, queer or inter-sectional) in anti-authoritarian communities in Berlin and Montreal. She is now working on justice practices that are de-veloped in feminist and antiracist social movements as altern-atives to criminal justice. She is also co-coordinator of the international French-speaking research network VisaGe, which focuses on gender-based violence.

Anna Kruzynski is a professor at the School of Community and Public Affairs and director of the Community Economy De-velopment program at Concordia University. She is a member of the TREEs collective, a self-managed research group that is mapping emancipatory economic practices proliferating on the margins of the social economy in so-called Québec using parti-cipatory action research. Her most recent field work and writ-ing is on autogestion and power at Building 7, a grassroots community-led hub of cooperatives and self-managed work-spaces that she helped bring into existence and develop over a period of 13 years. Her teaching is inspired by both her activism and her research. She teaches strategies for fundamental social change, economic literacy to enable people to take back the economy, basic community organizing skills and tools for dir-ect democracy.

Robert Lovelace teaches in the Department of Global Development Studies at Queen's University, Canada. His writing and activism have addressed issues related to human rights, environmental justice, and indigenous rights.

Miguel A. Martínez is Professor of Housing and Urban So-ciology at the IBF (Institute for Housing and Urban Research), Uppsala University (Sweden). His first interests focused on Par-ticipatory-Action-Research methods and processes. These were applied to the study of citizen participation in urban planning and urban movements. He mainly studies social movements and urban phenomena from a sociological perspective. His activist engagement encompasses squatting, housing, anti-austerity, migration and autonomist politics, mostly developed in Spain and across Europe. He was one of the founders of the activist-research network SqEK (Squatting Everywhere Kollective). He is the author of *Squatters in the Capitalist City* (Routledge, 2020), editor of *The Urban Politics of Squatters' Movements* (Palgrave, 2018), and co-editor of *Contested Cities and Urban Activism* (Palgrave, 2019). Most of his publications are freely available at: www.miguelangelmartinez.net

Rachel Sarrasin is a political science teacher at the undergraduate level in colleges in Québec. She has studied at Université du Québec à Montréal (UQAM), Universidad Nacional Autonoma de Mexico (UNAM) and Université de Montréal (UdeM), where she completed a Ph.D. in Political Science on antiauthoritarian organizing in Quebec at the turn of the 21st century. She was actively involved in various antiauthoritarian groups in Quebec during that time, including the Convergence des luttes anticapitalistes (CLAC) and the Collectif de recherche sur l'autonomie collective (CRAC). She has also been involved in the student, feminist, and labor movements.

AK Thompson got kicked out of high school for publishing an underground newspaper called *The Agitator* and has been an activist and social theorist ever since. He is the author and editor of numerous books, including *Black Bloc, White Riot: Anti-Globalization and the Genealogy of Dissent* (2010), *Spontaneous Combustion: The Eros Effect and Global Revolution,* and *Premonitions: Selected Essays on the Culture of Revolt* (2017).

Ask your local independent bookstore
for these titles or visit blackrosebooks.com

Eros and Revolution
George Katsiaficas

Paperback: 978-1-55164-809-5
Hardcover: 978-1-55164-811-8
eBook: 978-1-55164-813-2

Take the City:
Voices of Radical Municipalism
Jason Toney, ed.

Paperback: 978-1-55164-727-2
Hardcover: 978-1-55164-729-6
eBook: 978-1-55164-731-9

Common Futures:
Social Transformation and Political Ecology
Yavor Tarinski and Alexander Schismenos

Paperback: 978-1-55164-773-9
Hardcover: 978-1-55164-775-3
eBook: 978-1-55164-777-7

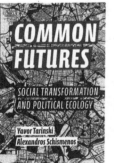

Montréal: A Citizen's Guide to City Politics
Mostafa Henaway, Jason Prince,
and Eric Shragge eds.

Paperback: 978-1-55164-779-1
Hardcover: 978-1-55164-781-4
eBook: 978-1-55164-780-7

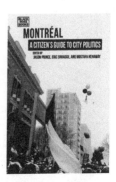